THE POWER
OF TOTAL
COMMITMENT

A LEADER'S LEGACY

Second Edition

FRANK WAGNER

The Power of Total Commitment

For information about this title or to order other books and/or electronic media, contact:
Marshall Goldsmith Stakeholder Centered Coaching
Coach@SCCoaching.com
www.SCCoaching.com

ISBN:
9780986324819 (print)
9780986324802 (e-book)

Printed in the United States of America

Dedication

*To all those whose commitment inspired this book,
especially my immediate family*

Contents

Preface for Second Edition vii

Foreword to First Edition by Ken Blanchard ix

Foreword to Second Edition by Jim Kouzes. xii

1. The Legacy of Commitment. 1

2. Focus on What's Important 4

3. Lead by Example 22

4. Reward Success 38

5. Manage Disrespect. 54

6. Focus on the Unimportant. 70

7. Follow the Lead 90

8. Challenge Success. 108

9. Be Disrespectful. 124

10. Uncharted Waters 140

Preface for Second Edition

The beginnings of this book go back to the early 1980s. Then, members of the management development staff at IBM asked Marshall Goldsmith, one of my partners, and me to develop a workshop building on the ideas found in McKinsey & Company's "Excellent Company Study." Out of this study an amazingly popular book was written titled *"In Search of Excellence"* by Tom Peters and Bob Waterman.

The best-selling book described the attributes of excellent companies that had achieved long-term success and status in the marketplace. This work seemed to indirectly offer insights into the actions of individual managers who worked inside these successful companies. Taking these ideas as a starting place, and using McKinsey's methodology of selecting companies with the best reputations for enduring success, we spent time with individual managers who had earned their own reputation for lasting success.

Based on the results of our analysis we developed a workshop for IBM called "The Excellent Manager." I am deeply indebted to Marshall for his partnership on this work. And, I cannot be more proud of what he has done for the profession of leadership development over the subsequent thirty years.

Also, with this project we were equally indebted to those managers we studied so many years ago. Their insights into leadership and the example they set in their own actions guided the development of the framework we uncovered. This early work helped pinpoint the half-dozen key commitments effective leaders consistently maintain.

Missing from our initial efforts was a simple framework linking these commitments together. At first, each commitment seemed to be achieved by a somewhat different set of behaviors. At the time I took on the task of writing up what we had come to realize were the underlying principles and practices of commitment, I relied heavily on the support of my two business partners, Chris Coffey and Gerry Rossy. Their support was instrumental in coming up with the contents of this book.

During the writing of this book, in the late 1980s, my undying gratitude goes out to my patient wife, Karen, who had to put up with all those hours sitting in front of my PC. Once ready for review, my wife and now deceased father were incredible at picking up not only the obvious mistakes but also the very subtle ones. My good friend, Father Bruno Segatta, painted the delightful original paintings that make this book worthwhile in their own right. Bruno, to this day, is a truly gifted artist. He has the talent to paint a picture in many media, whether on canvas, clay, or conversation.

Ken Blanchard, in his usual style, was a great role model for everything from how to get an idea across to what ideas to have in the first place. Ken is a giant in this field because of who he is as a person. How blessed could someone be to meet him when I was getting started in the field of leadership. I am indebted to him for writing the foreword to the first edition of this book.

Jim Kouzes, like Ken, is a rare breed who not only has the scholarship and insight needed to be a contributor at the highest level in our field of leadership, but he is also a genuine example of what is a leader in his own actions. Jim was equally kind to write the foreword to this second edition of the book.

Foreword to First Edition

When Frank Wagner asked me to read his manuscript, the first thing it reminded me of was a deeply held belief I have formed from years of practical experience. Many of the crises we face today in our personal and professional growth are not due to lack of leadership...they are based on a lack of commitment. We have done a pretty good job of teaching leadership and influence skills over the past few decades. We have done a much poorer job in the area of commitment.

Commitment is one of the most important things we can possess. It is also an easy thing to recognize in people. Looking inward we also have a pretty good sense of when we are committed and when we are not. When we stop to think about how we actually demonstrate our commitments, here is where things become much more complex. This is where *The Power of Total Commitment* comes in handy. It helps build a perspective and understanding of this critical component to success. We all live up to our commitments to some degree. The lessons from this book reinforce what we now do well. Each chapter also points out what may be missing from our own behavior.

The method Frank uses to help introduce these important lessons is in the form of a story. Anyone who knows me and my work knows this is my preferred way to present a message. In the tradition of the *One Minute*

Manager that I co-authored with Spencer Johnson, and *The Power of Ethical Management* which I wrote with Norman Vincent Peale, this program is a contemporary, adult allegory. It is a parable. Many of the principles from my work in helping people to grow can be found in this refreshing perspective on commitment. This pleases me immensely. Although the setting may cause the reader to think this a management book, it is a far cry more. The lessons from this parable apply equally well to family, business, community and oneself. To achieve lasting success in our lives we must faithfully live up to our commitment to ourselves and others.

Let me give you an example from my own personal life. I remember saying to a friend, Fred Finch, one time, "Fred, I wish I was more organized." Fred replied, "Ken, you are the most organized person I know when you're committed to do something. You probably beat yourself up because you aren't committed to do everything and yet you think you should be."

And, I thought about that—that is really interesting! Commitment is when you say that you're going to do what you said you were going to do and you follow through. But, you can't be committed to everything. I remember at that point I was beating myself up because I wasn't losing weight and it was a very busy time. I said to myself, "…you know what, I'm not going to commit about doing something about my weight right now." That was a big relief. We all want to personally experience a strong sense of commitment in our lives, and we get frustrated when we do not keep our commitments.

How about organizations? I do a lot of work for organizations and I also see the main issue there as commitment. For example, I get 150 or so annual reports every year from various companies we have worked with. And, in every report on the first page, there is a mention that without customers we would be nothing. The customers are the key to our success. Also, within a paragraph or so is always a statement that without our people we would be nothing. People, the people who work for us, are our most important resource. So, customers and people are getting the headlines in every organization.

When I go into these companies I'll say, "I see you're committed to your customers and your people. Do you mind if I look at your management practices to see if you are really walking your talk? Are you keeping your commitment to your customers and people?" And, it's amazing how people become stutterers and really get upset because they aren't walking their talk. I am convinced that organizations can be just as good as they dream of being if they keep their commitments. So, I think commitment, and what Frank is talking about, is so important for success in our lives and in our companies.

Ken Blanchard

Foreword to Second Edition

A few years ago I was on a panel with management educator and author, Ken Blanchard, who wrote the foreword to this book's first edition. I was responding to an audience member's question, and I began by saying, "I don't know what you call something that's been the same for twenty-five years, but…." Before I could finish my sentence Ken interrupted, exclaiming, "I'd call it the truth."

Ken's witty observation was spot on, and his comment reinforced that some things about leadership are so valid and consistent—and don't change that much over time—that they deserve to be called what they are, *the truth*.

That is exactly the reaction I had in reading Frank Wagner's book, *The Power of Total Commitment*. While the first edition of this book was published a number of years ago, its messages are as fresh and as true today as they were when Frank originally told the story of Art, a recently retired CEO, and Sam, his protégé and new CEO. *The Power of Total Commitment* has stood the test of time. And, as the demographics of the workplace shift from Boomers to GenXers to Millennials, and as organizations become ever more diverse, these lessons seem downright prescient.

Three truths in particular stand out for me in reading Frank's new edition.

The first truth is that **values drive commitment**. People want to know what you stand for and believe in. They want to know your values and beliefs, what you really care about, and what keeps you awake at night. They want to know who most influenced you, the events that shaped your attitudes, and the experiences that prepare you for the job. They want to know what drives you, what makes you happy, and what ticks you off. They want to know what you're like as a person, and why you want to be their leader. They want to know if you play an instrument, compete in sports, go to the movies, or enjoy the theater. They want to know about your family, what you've done, and where you've traveled. They want to understand your personal story. They want to know why they ought to be following you.

Values represent the core of who you are, and values are at the heart of Frank's book. It's where he begins because he knows that everything flows from there. Commitment, as Frank defines it, is about believing in something and then acting consistent with that belief. As Art tells Sam, "The ability to focus on what's important is essential to effective leadership and management."

It's impossible to fully commit to something that isn't important to you. You can't fully commit to something that doesn't fit with who you are and how you see yourself. In order to devote the time, to expend the energy, and to make the sacrifices necessary you have to know exactly what makes it worth doing in the first place.

Becoming a leader is a process of self-discovery. And, it's the first part of Sam's journey with Art. He helps Sam realize that there are a lot of different interests out there competing for your time, your attention, and your approval. Before you listen to those voices, you have to listen to that voice inside that tells you what's truly important.

The second truth I was reminded of when reading *The Power of Commitment* is that **you either lead by example, or you don't lead at all.** It's what Sam learns in the second session with Art. My good friend and coauthor, Barry Posner, and I discovered early on in our research that *credibility is the foundation of leadership*. People have to believe in you if they are going to willingly follow you. People can't commit to a leader who isn't credible. And, what is credibility behaviorally? When we asked this question, the answer came back loud and clear: You must *do what you say you will do.*

Seeing is believing, and your constituents have to see you living out the standards you've set and the values you profess. You need to go first in setting the example for others. A big part of leading by example is keeping your promises. Your word is only as good as your actions. You have to realize that others look to you and your actions in order to determine for themselves how serious you are about what you say, as well as understanding what it will mean for them to be "walking the talk." Your statements and actions are visible reminders to others about what is or is not important. As Sam says, "I realized no one escapes from leading by example. The only question is, what example are we setting? Is it the one we really want, or do our actions reflect what really isn't all that important?"

Sam and Art develop a deep and binding relationship over the course of this book, and there are many other lessons that Sam learns on this voyage of self-discovery. Yet, it is this journey itself that highlights the third truth about which I was reminded. The truth is that **the best leaders are the best learners**.

Over the years Barry and I have conducted a series of empirical studies to find out if leaders could be differentiated by the range and depth of learning tactics they employ. We wanted to know if the way leaders learned played a role in how effective they were in leading. The results have been most intriguing. First, we found that leadership can be learned in a variety of ways. It can be learned through active experimentation, observation of others, study in the classroom or reading books, or simply reflecting on one's own and others' experiences. Certain styles contribute to more effectiveness in some practices, but there is no one best style for learning everything there is to know. The style was not the thing.

What was more important was the extent to which individuals engaged in whatever style worked for them. Those leaders who were more engaged in each of their learning styles, regardless of what their styles were, scored higher on practices of exemplary leadership. The best leaders turned out to be the best learners.

These findings also raise a very important question: Which comes first, learning or leading? Whenever we ask our clients this question, their hunches are the same as ours. Learning comes first. When people are predisposed to be curious and want to learn something new, they are much more likely to get better at it than those who don't become fully engaged.

Learning is the master skill. When you fully engage in learning—when you throw yourself whole-heartedly into experimenting, reflecting, reading, or getting coaching—you are going to experience the kind of growth that Sam experiences on his journey with Art.

You can develop yourself as a leader, but it takes a continuous personal investment. It takes time, it takes deliberate practice, it requires setting improvement goals, staying open to feedback, working on your strengths and weaknesses, and having the support of others—someone like Sam, for instance.

Now join in that journey with Sam as he puts this truth into practice. As Art tells him, "All experience offers some lesson." The experience of reading this book will offer you many lessons.

Jim Kouzes

Coauthor of *The Leadership Challenge* & *The Truth About Leadership*

The real test of business greatness lies in
giving opportunity to others.

— Charles Schwab

Chapter 1
THE LEGACY OF COMMITMENT

The seclusion of the house hidden behind the gateway was just as I remembered. Situated on a level mesa high in the foothills, this was the kind of estate that offers a spectacular panorama of the countryside below. Yet, the property remains virtually invisible to those curious about what lies within.

Seeing the intricate ironwork on the gate reminded me of the purpose of my visit here tonight. It's puzzling to me why I am so different. The loyalty I've felt for him has been longstanding. I felt it before I ever met him. His reputation was good enough for me from the beginning. That was over twenty years ago. Once I actually worked with him, my feelings grew even stronger.

As I drove through the gateway toward the main house, I felt a need to unravel the mystery of how I had managed to make it this far. Walking through the lush grounds toward the entrance to the house was not the pleasure it should have been. The landscape, a mixture of man's creative enhancement to nature's own choices, made a lovely diversion for the wandering eye.

For better or worse, my steps along the path were filled with anticipation and trepidation. I was much too preoccupied to enjoy the passage to the front door. I was thinking about the invitation to visit the *old man*. He founded the company I now ran.

One can acquire everything in solitude,
except character.

— Henri Beyle

Chapter 2

FOCUS ON WHAT'S IMPORTANT

Just over a year ago, Art surprised everyone. At the age of fifty-eight he announced he would retire in a year's time. He had built a major corporation from his own vision and hard work. Upon retirement, he selected me as his successor. What led him to this decision was still puzzling to me. I felt surprised, humbled, and honored to be offered the job.

Why me? Would I find out tonight? When I took over, he gave no explanation for his decision. Worse yet, he left without a word of guidance. All he told me was he believed in me and would not interfere in my running the business. That was three months ago. During that time he was true to his word. For all practical purposes, he disappeared. Now, without warning, he sent word he wanted me to have dinner at his house.

After being escorted out to the back patio, I saw Art leaning on the railing. He was staring out at the valley below. After a warm greeting, he offered me a drink. Then we sat down so we could talk and enjoy the view.

"Where's Marilyn?" was my first question.

"Oh, she's in Portland visiting some of our grandchildren."

"Art, I'm a bit surprised you're not up there, too."

"I'm heading up there tomorrow. I just couldn't shift a meeting I've been asked to attend. When you volunteer on the board of a charity, it's not right to duck out unless it's really some kind of an emergency. And, by staying it also gave me an opportunity to have a chat with you."

"So, when it comes to the grandchildren, I suppose Marilyn's not patient enough to wait for you?"

"You can say that again. I think she's happy to spend time with them without having to put up with my shenanigans. Speaking of spouses, I'd have invited Kris if Marilyn had been home. Since she's gone, I felt it would make more sense if just the two of us met."

"Fine by me."

"How's the family anyway? Are they adjusting to living with a Chief Executive Officer?

"Hasn't seemed to impress any of them. I'm just as glad. Everything is wonderful at home. The kids are doing great at school. Kris's freelance business is beginning to take off. And, really, I think they're all excited about my promotion."

Between cocktails and the start of dinner, we spent a good deal of time swapping stories about our families. Dinner itself went as I expected. I knew Art wouldn't talk business during the meal. This was one of his rules. Life, to him, was far more diverse than talking shop all the time. He felt conversation was one of the best forms of entertainment. I never forgot he once told me his favorite movie was *My Dinner With Andre*.

On his recommendation I went to see the movie myself. It amazed me I could be entertained for over two hours by a movie where the only action was a conversation between two people I didn't know. Now I was caught in a similar script. Yet, mine was real.

I knew him well, having reported directly to him for a number of years. However, in many respects, I felt there was a lot about this man I didn't know. If it weren't for his charm and intelligence, I would have suffered during the wait until dinner was finished and we could go into the study.

I wanted to bring up business. Yet, if I brought up anything to do with work while we ate, he'd have politely cut me off with something like, "There's always time to talk about business...let's talk about...," and he'd change the topic. I knew it was pointless to try and steer the conversation to business, so I didn't try.

As it was, I found myself lost in conversation about the differences between amateur and professional sports to comparing today's youth with those of prior generations. At one point we talked about favorite movies. His three favorites were a strange combination: *Butch Cassidy and the Sundance Kid*, *The Wizard of Oz*, and *My Dinner with Andre*. When he explained why he loved these films, I found myself marveling at the meaning he could glean from what for me was simply entertainment.

When we finally moved to his well-appointed library, I knew the time was right to shift the conversation to business. "I've been watching you closely over the last three months, Sam," he said as I sat down in an overstuffed leather chair near the fire.

"Even though I don't know how you have done that, it doesn't surprise me. You said something to the same effect after announcing my appointment as CEO."

"You're right about that," he chuckled. "Your career has interested me since the first year you started working with us."

I didn't try to hide my puzzled look and figured I might as well voice my curiosity. "Why me, Art? Why did you pick me as your successor?"

"Simple...you showed promise from the beginning. Within your first year as a manager, you showed you had the right stuff. Now I know you've been dying to ask me why you were chosen. Thanks for your patience. As you might expect, the question of 'why you' isn't easy to answer. So, please bear with me. Let me start by saying I'm glad you brought this up because the answer to your question is the main reason I suggested we get together tonight."

"Go on," I invited. "You've got my undivided attention."

Exhaling slowly, he began. "Okay, I purposely kept my distance as you took over the leadership role. I wanted you to have as much room to maneuver without any interference from my end. It is important that you are seen as not my understudy. You need to make your own mark on the company. Being on your own is also a good way to get a feel for what is in store for you."

He went on to say, "Now that you've been in the top spot for a little while, I want to talk with you about the qualities that led me to select you as my successor. Although I never felt any other candidate was a serious competitor to you, we did have some well-qualified options open to us."

"You are definitely right about that, Art. Personally, I might have bet on Bart Freeman. He certainly was an obvious choice to me. He's always been a top performer. I can't think of any weaknesses to disqualify him. I would have been happy to have reported to him…I'm still not clear why me instead of Bart."

"Because you, more faithfully than Bart, demonstrated the kind of commitment I expect."

Finding myself on the edge of the chair I asked, "And, what kind of commitment is that?"

Looking me right in the eye, he replied, "You persist in making the right things happen. I like referring to it as *persistence with a purpose*. And…you have it in spades. Throughout your entire career with us I never saw you waiver from doing the right thing. And, what makes this such a compliment to you is you certainly had your challenges."

Agreeing I said, "I have had a few sleepless nights for sure."

"Sam, you've represented the company in some crucial areas and through some rough times. You may not want to have to do a repeat performance. None of us do. But, as far as I'm concerned it's good you've been tested. It made my selection a whole lot easier. I always liked Thomas Edison's line about success being 1 percent inspiration and 99 percent perspiration. Maybe you felt all that perspiration meant you weren't qualified for the job. In truth, it's the opposite."

What he said made me feel good. Yet, I still didn't feel I had a tangible answer as to why me. "Sure, I've got determination. I know that. Yet, Bart is no different. And, I'd say the same for the rest of the management team. Yet, none of them got the job. I did."

"Your persistence was different. Yours contained an element of focus that all the others lacked."

I was getting a glimmer of what was driving Art's decision. I felt it. Yet, I still couldn't put my finger on what he was driving at. So, I decided to pick up on what he had said about persistence, "Let me backtrack a bit to what you said earlier. When you mentioned commitment, you called it persistence with a purpose. Could you elaborate?"

"You bet! To me commitment really requires two things. First, you have to believe in something. A prerequisite for commitment is a sense of direction. Without something of importance, something you fundamentally buy into, you lack one of the key ingredients of commitment. This applies to everyone.

I wish I didn't have to say this, but there are people who just drift with no real sense of purpose or direction. Having something to believe in is vital to commitment. And, it's also only half of what it takes. The second necessity for commitment is the tougher part. Namely, you also need the willingness to persist and act consistent with what you believe in over the long haul. If you want a concrete measure of commitment, use time.

How consistently and faithfully you practice your beliefs over time is the truest test and best measure of commitment. You see, Sam, we all know there are a lot of ambitious people with drive, determination and persistence. Yet not nearly as many can be described as having both the focus and consistency needed to demonstrate genuine commitment."

"So the way you see commitment is over the long term?"

"It is the person who maintains his or her commitment over the long haul that I respect. And, as far as you're concerned, this kind of person I reward." After a short pause, he added, "Is this helpful? Are you beginning to understand why you wound up being my choice?"

I had to admit I was feeling pretty good about myself as he talked. Living up to the standards Art was describing seemed quite an accomplishment. The bottom line is that I did feel I lived up to what he said. However, my response was still a bit hesitant, "Yes, I am beginning to get a clearer picture. It's just I'm not sure I'm 100 percent trustworthy."

Art threw me with his next question. "How would you describe me when I was in your office? When I was the CEO?"

Thinking about it for a second I said, "Honestly, I felt you could do no wrong. I always banked on the belief that the *old man* always came through for all of us. It was comforting knowing you were in the job…I can truly say you never let me down. Now that I have to take up where you left off, I'm feeling you are that proverbial act no one wants to have to follow."

Chuckling, he responded, "Sounds like I was perfect. Let me tell you, during all those years I felt no different than you appear to be at this moment. Questioning yourself and your ability to succeed is natural. So is wanting a perfect track record."

As this surprised me a bit I admitted, "You could have fooled me. You never gave a hint you weren't in total control…the image of confidence."

"That's because I learned a long time ago of the power of commitment. I also discovered that many of your failures go unnoticed, and those that are can usually be turned into success stories if you approach them with the strength of your commitments. I want to get back to something you just said, Sam. Unless I'm reading you wrong, you said you're a bit unsure of your ability to follow me in the role of chief executive. It's natural. I was in the job a long time. Everyone knew what to expect from me."

"Yes, as comfortable as an old broken-in pair of jeans."

"You, on the other hand, are new. I don't care how good someone is, there is a period of time when expectations have to be established, accepted, and demonstrated. It's the nature of such transitions. These will be the most awkward times you'll face. If you handle the challenges it becomes a whole lot easier.

My goal is you make sure you continue in the ways that made you my first choice. You deserve to know what it is I admire about you. Our getting together has nothing to do with my faith in your competence to lead our business in the years ahead. What I'm curious enough about to ask, and the reason I invited you over tonight, is to find out how conscious you are of what you do so effectively."

As Art talked I wanted to tell him his curiosity about all this—the decision to make me the CEO—what makes me tick, what made him such a great leader—all paled in comparison to my own. I felt he saw in me what he held dear in himself. How comforting to think there were certain characteristics common between us.

I always liked the idea of being compared to him. He cast such a long shadow. I'd like to think I could do as well some day. From the first day I met Art I admired the guy. I pondered whether this was the right time to tell him. As I was about to, he interrupted my thoughts with a question.

"What commitments do you feel are necessary for a leader to have?"

Responding a bit too quickly I said, "Obviously, our customers deserve our full commitment. Likewise a commitment to our people is essential." After mentioning these two I noticeably slowed down, as I wanted to ensure I answered appropriately.

Art prodded me by asking, "And what links our people to our customers?"

"The services we provide. So it follows, there needs to be strong commitment to what it is we do, the results we are striving to attain as a company." As I talked Art picked up a piece of paper off his desk. On the top he wrote the word *Commitment*. After that he began drawing what appeared to be some sort of diagram.

Watching him construct this figure, I noticed he first drew a square that was rotated forty-five degrees where the edges of the square pointed to the middle of each side of the paper. The diagram was positioned right in the middle of the page below the word *Commitment*.

"You've mentioned Customers, Results, and People. Did I also hear you mention the Company?"

"Sure," I responded. "The Organization a leader works for is certainly important."

While I answered, Art wrote *Customer* over the top of the rotated square. On the other three points he scrawled *Results*, *People*, and *Organization*.

Looking up at me, he said, "Sam, I'm not quite satisfied with your answer yet. Let me ask you another question if I may...What is the most important part of your current job as you see it?"

Many years ago, Art had given a memorable speech at the annual board meeting. At that time, he described his role as the CEO in quite simple terms. As I remember it, he described his job as preserving the values of the organization, making sure we lived up to them. I never forgot his words. Before then I'd thought his job was so multifaceted that it defied definition.

During that speech I had come to two important conclusions. First, for all the different directions the CEO could be tugged, he still had a relatively straightforward and simple task, when defined in terms of our *Value Statement*. It was comforting to see a man so versatile and so focused. Second, and much more meaningful to me, I realized that my job wasn't a lot different from the CEO's. I saw myself as one manager who, if I helped preserve the values we stood for, would best serve everyone, including myself.

"Art, the most important part of my job is to keep our two basic values alive and well. I've got to make sure every new employee knows them, every current employee remembers them, and we all live by them daily. If I do that, we have the critical mass of talent to take care of the rest."

Pleasure filled his face as he nodded agreement. Almost inaudibly, he whispered, "Exactly." Then, with building excitement he exclaimed, "Every single success we've had came when we acted consistently with our core values. Failure occurred when we lost sight of them. I learned a long time ago you're much better off stating what you believe so everyone knows what you stand for.

How we are viewed in the marketplace is built on our two basic values: Be a *Leader in Quality* and *Integrity in every Business Relationship*. I found these points to be sound principles to ground a service business on."

"Couldn't agree more! It is why I chose to come work here over the other offers I was given. What impressed me about the Company was the reputation lived up to your stated values."

I noticed Art was writing something in the middle of the box he had drawn earlier. It was the word *Values*. I felt dumb I hadn't immediately mentioned this when he first asked what commitments are important for a leader. After writing *Values*, Art busily and carefully drew arrows at each corner of the box. When finished, he turned the page around so I could see it right side up for the first time. As I scanned the figure, Art spoke to me with a reflective tone.

"You've demonstrated our values in your business practices as well as I ever did. Remember earlier I said commitment requires focus. Given all the seemingly important issues that tug at and compete for our time, you have to be able to ferret out what is key. Once you do that you have to devote your energies to making sure those precious, truly important things get done.

There's always plenty to do," he chuckled. "The ability and skill to *focus on what's important* is essential to effective leadership and management. What you see in this simple drawing is where an effective leader practices commitment. You have served all of these exceedingly well in the various roles we have put you in over the years."

"Maybe I have. Yet, I guess it really boils down to being true to yourself. I really do believe in what you've drafted here. Bottom line, it boils down to integrity. I buy into what you have stood for since you started our company."

"You've just hit on something I haven't thought of before. Give me back the paper, please."

Not exactly sure what I had triggered in Art's thinking, I was intrigued by what he would add to his drawing. Right underneath

Values, in the middle of the figure, he added *Self.* Once again he turned the paper to my point of view.

"You know, Sam, what drives your commitment to others stems from a clear commitment to your own integrity and following up on what you believe. Personally I was overjoyed with your answer that the CEO's job focuses on keeping our values alive and well. It is just the kind of thing I'd expect you to say."

As Art talked, I began to think about all the decisions I had made over the years. The pressure of short-term performance goals to achieve needed short-term profit often had driven fundamental principles like integrity and quality of service from my conscious choices. Yet, whenever I got into a bind, whenever I couldn't quite decide which way to go, whenever it became sweaty-palms time, those values always somehow surfaced and helped me make up my mind.

They seemed to pop into my head at the right moment and guide my choices. I realized, however, I hadn't always given our Core Values the priority they deserved. This recognition made me ask Art the following question:

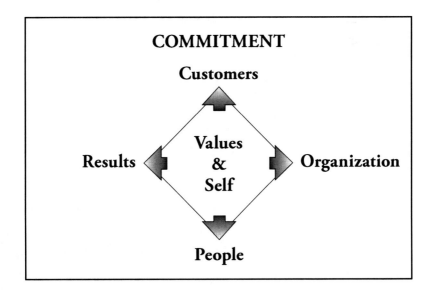

"Art, you taught me most of the insights I possess about my job. I truly believe my fundamental task is to inject a continuing dose of our values to the people who work with us. But, I'm not sure my record is all that pure. There are times I got sidetracked. It's so easy to get distracted. How do you, or anyone for that matter, keep properly focused?"

"I'm not sure how others keep focused. For me, it is quite simple. First, put to memory what's important. It may seem odd to you, but even I had to make a conscious effort to remember our two Core Values. Second, I had them printed up and placed in a conspicuous spot in my office where I could see them. There was nothing better than a physical reminder to keep what's important prominent in my thinking. Third, I developed a set of key questions for myself. I ask myself these questions daily. Made up what I call a daily checklist. At the end of the day I have a ritual where I scan the questions quickly and ask myself if my actions lived up to what I expect of myself."

Unable to contain myself I interrupted and asked: "And, what were those questions?"

Tapping the paper where he had drawn the commitments, he explained, "Whenever I found myself with a choice, whether a complex business decision involving the whole company or simply responding to an individual, the way I wanted to act was to be effective AND consistent relative to our commitments. So, at the end of the day I'd ask:

1. Did I help our customers today?
2. Did I help in achieving any of our key results?
3. Did I help our people today?
4. Did I help our Company's mission and strategy?
5. Was I a good role model of our Company's values?

If the answer to these questions was yes, I left feeling good about the day. If the answer to any of these questions was 'no,' I spent some time doing a post mortem and how I could do better the next day."

As he described his routine to me I found myself wishing I could take notes. There was simplicity to what he was describing. There was also a lot of discipline involved. It always amazed me that I needed to learn the same lesson over and over again. It became apparent to me the ease with which Art wove his values into his own life and that of the company was possible because of all the hard work that took place under the surface.

Discipline and hard work often seem to be the predecessor of what looks so natural and easy. I envisioned the time it took for him to make his questioning routine second nature. I bet he thought about those questions during the day and not just at the end when he was doing his end-of-the-day assessment. My mind wandered to my own rather sloppy, haphazard way of doing what he so eloquently described.

"Do you think I could improve my focus by employing your methods?"

An enthusiastic "Of course you can!" came from Art. Then he added, "I've never considered any methods of achieving results sophisticated. Plain wrapped is more like it. There's nothing difficult about what I set out to accomplish. The only truly hard part was the persistence required. I found every day I had to ask myself if I was spending my time on what was truly necessary. That is why I got in the habit, while shaving in the morning, of asking myself, "What do I have to do today if I'm going to focus on what's important?"

I had to nod in agreement as Art described his regimen in front of the mirror. I find the early morning a good time for reflection too. Like Art's shaving in the mirror, I usually spend a few quiet moments mapping out my day as I give my dog a short walk around my neighborhood.

Before I could take any comfort in this thought, a new unsettling thought entered my mind. How often do others dictate our schedule? How often is our agenda at the mercy of others? How often does scope creep crowd out what is important?

"Can you, as CEO, really dictate what you do and where you spend your time?"

"Certainly no one is in complete control over their schedule...AND, it is also true that it is your company to run. Isn't it?"

"I know that. But, my God, the line of people at the door with valid claims on my time and energy is daunting. Just the list of events a CEO has to attend..."

"I'm sorry if I made this sound simple," he apologized. "There are a lot of well-intended people who will steer you off course if you let them. What I found extremely useful, yet painful to do, was to ask another question. Whenever you find yourself off your game plan, this question cuts to the heart of the matter.

What question am I talking about? Simply, *is this worth doing?* Surely this question does not come as a surprise. It is a question I'd quickly ask others out loud if my own answer was 'It's not worth doing.' The purpose of the question is two-fold. First, it makes others think about the matter. Second, it gives another perspective. Maybe it is worth the time and effort and I'm not seeing it right...Now, just to test if I'm pontificating I want you to think back to how many times I asked YOU this question?"

Unable to suppress a smile I had to admit, "Enough!...Part of your reputation was being direct. I remember whenever I wasn't fully prepared and started stalling, you'd always catch me with one of your questions. Is this really worth doing wasn't the only question you used. I recall you seemed also fond of 'Is there a better way?' These questions really taught me to have my act together. I never liked it when I was unable to respond fully, or was wasting precious time when there were more important things to do."

Listening thoughtfully Art then asked me, "And, what was the purpose of those questions I'd ask you so often?"

"I figured it was to keep me focused on what was important."

"You're half right. I also asked those questions to help ME stay focused."

As he spoke, I began to marvel at his insight. I had always seen his questions as helping me think through important issues. I never considered he was facilitating his own thinking at the same time. I guess if you're aware that you can easily get sidetracked, you're humble enough to keep asking yourself, over and over again, the basic questions.

Breaking into my thought process, he interjected, "One more thing, I found it very helpful to make a short list of my priorities. I worked to keep the list under a dozen items. Obviously, the first item on my list was *maintain our values*. Besides our values, I included the commitments and searched for one or two key actions I could take to ensure I was 70 percent to 80 percent successful at fulfilling each one."

"Is this list available?"

"Maybe some day. Now is not the right time. There is real value for you going through the process of creating your own list."

Even though I intellectually understood his point, I'd give just about anything to see what he had come up with. Reluctantly, I conceded half-heartedly, "I can live with that." As I said this, I thought of something, "Did your list change over time?"

"Good question," Art replied.

"The actions on this list are not static. The list can change over time and deserves constant review. To answer your question, yes, it did change—but not much. Sometimes different items took on more significance. Yet, everything on the list was important. This list served two useful purposes. First, I would get an instant review of my performance since last looking at it. Second, by scanning the list, I would gain a perspective for what I needed to do next."

"Looks like I've got a list to construct."

"I'm glad you see it that way." Tapping the picture he had created on the paper, he continued, "The only advice I'll give you is to make sure each commitment is represented somewhere on your list. Work hard at coming up with the one or two things you want to do continually to enhance our customers, our key results, our employees, the organization's overall mission and strategy, and most importantly, our values."

Art pointed out the hour was late. Knowing the night would have to end sometime, I wasn't prepared to let it happen so soon. After months without him, I wanted to pick Art's brain for as long as he'd let me.

I pushed for a little more time. He was agreeable, inviting me to ask him whatever was on my mind. I brought up business issues facing the company. I wanted his opinion on how to handle these situations. He freely gave advice in the areas where I needed it. After graciously extending our time past my request for another forty-five minutes, Art again suggested we call it a night. He then added, "I appreciated the chance to get together. It meant a lot to me, and I'd like to do it again. How would you like to get together once a month for awhile?"

My immediate response was, "Great! You tell me the time and place and I'll be there. It's weird saying this since you've taught me so much over the years, but I feel there is still a lot to learn…important things… things you have stored inside that graying head of yours."

"I'm not so sure there's all that much left in this graying head you don't already know," he replied. "Tonight you showed me more than you probably know about yourself. Why I'd like to meet over the months ahead is to simply help place some finishing touches on the enormous talent you have built up over years. My main goal in asking you here tonight was to find out what you think is most important in your job. To say I am pleased with your response is an understatement. If there is one thing I want you to take away tonight, it's the necessity of keeping focused on what's important."

As he talked, he scribbled a note and handed it to me. On the paper were just four words: *focus on what's important.* "Remember, Sam, your key responsibility is to keep the values functioning in the organization. That job permeates everything you do. However, in addition to the values, specific day-to-day events and activities are also important. Focusing on what's important isn't easy. Know why?"

"I'd say…because there are usually a number of important things requiring your attention. In the conduct of business, you know as well as I do, priorities change."

"In light of this fact, what makes conducting business easier is keeping in mind that you're devoting yourself to what's most important at any given time. My best advice for you is do your best to keep your job simple."

"I know what you mean. Most people need clearer and fewer objectives to truly succeed in their jobs."

"For reasons not clear to me, organizational dynamics seem at odds with whatever is simple. There is a constant force making things more complex, requiring us to do more and more. Whatever is simple is made difficult with a subtle, methodical precision. Left unguarded you can bet what people are asked to do will get more complicated."

"So, what we've been talking about tonight—namely focus—is this your best defense?"

"That's right, Sam. Those with focus have a weapon in this war between simplicity and complexity. All of us have to aim for a simple vision. Some people think this has something to do with seeing the big picture. My experience says just the opposite. It's more closely aligned with focusing on what's vital and essential. You hear of people who come up with elegantly simple solutions to intricate and multifaceted problems. These are people armed with a clear and simple understanding of what's important. This is the secret of their ability to see past details and target what matters."

Art made me feel good with his final remark, "What is so appealing about your response to my main question tonight is you showed me you really do have what it takes to lead. As the CEO, you can never be too far off the mark if what you're doing supports our values. I'm proud to hear you answer with so much wisdom. Having the focus, knowing what is important, is a gift. Don't lose it."

As he walked me to the front door, he talked of our future meetings. We agreed to meet in the middle of October. He would take care of the details. There was a strong sense of friendship in our goodnight handshake. When I turned on the ignition, I realized how preoccupied I had been when I first arrived. I habitually turn off the music I'm listening to before shutting off the engine. When the music came on

I realized I hadn't stuck to my usual regimen. On my way here, I had been listening to Frontier Theory, a young group I had just discovered. Driving down the winding driveway past the front gate, I found myself caught by the lines of their song:

> But one left and one stayed.
> Let go of the one that got away.

I tried summing up the evening. The relevancy of those lines made me smile. Before my meeting with Art, I would have simply enjoyed the music. Now I was looking for a deeper meaning. As this cut from their album finished, I found myself reflecting on the evening. What came immediately to mind was commitment. I think the word *commitment* came up because that's how I felt. I suddenly remembered the last lines of Ken Blanchard's *Putting The One Minute Manager To Work*: "Keep your commitment to your commitment. And share it with others."

Tomorrow I'd be back at my desk in the CEO's office. I felt a revived and stronger sense of commitment to the tasks at hand. Art always made me feel this way. The man was a magician. He always seemed to have a plan, some grand design. And, I knew he wasn't finished with me yet. I wondered what he had in store for me next time.

Be careful how you live. You may be the only Bible some person ever reads.

— William J. Tom

Chapter 3
LEAD BY EXAMPLE

October arrived. A time of year I always liked. The weather was warm—Indian summer. Business looked good and I was settling into my routine as CEO. When I entered my office one Wednesday, I spotted a small envelope on top of my mail stack. Marcie, my executive secretary, usually sorts the mail. She puts important documents on top. Knowing both me and the CEO's job well, she has a good sense of what deserves attention. Art's return address on the envelope was the only clue she had to see. I opened his letter and read his invitation:

> *Sam,*
> *I'd like to do something different than dinner at my place again. Why don't we meet a week from Saturday at 8:00 a.m. Bring your bike and gear. We can make a morning of it and get a bit of exercise. If this doesn't fit your fancy, give me a ring. Otherwise, I'll see you in about a week.*
>
> > *Warmest regards,*
> > *Art*

p.s. First, I hope you've been focusing on what's important. Second, I want you to consider the following question: How can you get others to focus on what's most important?

So he wanted to meet on Saturday. Usually I refuse to tie up the weekend with business meetings. My weekends are reserved for family. On the other hand, I do allow time for a workout. I guess it would be okay to accept. As I put down the letter I had to chuckle. Conformity was never Art's style. Biking. That was interesting. I knew he was an avid cycler.

In the last few years he had been cross training, working out in a variety of sports. Personally, cycling was one of my strengths. When I was younger, I raced in team-relay, single-stage competition. Knowing how competitive Art was, I had to wonder how seriously he was training. I could see him pedaling furiously and endlessly just to show me he could keep up.

On second thought, Art wouldn't do that. Unless retirement is getting him down, he's got nothing to prove to himself, let alone me. I wonder why he wants to go riding? Then it hit me. Here I was caught up fantasizing about our upcoming bike ride. What I was ignoring was the most important part of his note, the question in the p.s.

After our last meeting, I took the paper on which Art had written *focus on what's important* and set it on my desk in front of the pen set. I wanted a visual reminder of what we talked about. Thankfully, many times a day Art's advice stared at me. This small scrap of paper helped me realize how easy it is to get sidetracked, just like reading the letter I was currently holding in my hand. My mind raced to the thought of riding instead of to the question Art posed in his letter. It's so easy to go where you want to go, where you enjoy going. Not so easy to head where your time is best spent.

Rereading the letter, I analyzed my performance. How well had I kept the right focus? For the most part, I'd been pretty successful. For instance, some of our key customers grumbled that we were less responsive to their needs than we'd been in the past. I then spent several weeks working with our service people and those customers to make sure our well-earned reputation remained a good one. The successful resolution of this problem was vital to the company.

The second part of the p.s. Art had put in the form of a question: "How can you get others to focus on what's most important?" My first inclination was not to answer the question, but to figure out why he was asking it. Was he trying to subtly make a point? Was this a gentle nudge that my job included getting everyone else to keep his or her goals in sight? Was he looking for me to arrive on Saturday with the *best* way?

After pondering these questions for a while, I came to the conclusion it was more productive to assume the answer to all three was "yes". After that insight, it seemed logical to get down to his actual question. The phone rang. It was Marcie. She told me in a few more minutes I had to leave for a presentation across town. There were a few things I needed to get done before heading out. Art's question would have to wait until later.

The rest of the day was jam packed with meetings and issues. It wasn't until after my teenagers were through with their demands that evening that I was able to get back to Art's question. Seated comfortably in my favorite chair, I began thinking about how to ensure those around me were keeping themselves focused on what's most important. I started listing ways in my head. First, there was the obvious answer—tell them. If people don't know what's important, you can't expect them to keep their priorities straight. Second, there was the use of reinforcement. You could reward people for keeping themselves pointed in the right direction. And, you could correct them when they fell off course.

I stalled after these first few ideas. I began repeating myself, coming up with the same responses. Nothing new came to me. All I was doing was refining the answers I already knew. Like a spinning top heading nowhere, I couldn't break free of the pattern I was in.

I had been thinking so hard I was shocked by how successfully I'd blocked out the music playing in the background. Relaxing, I decided to drift to the rhythm. My attention wandered back to my competitive cycling days. Almost every time I reminisced about those *good ole days* one person came to mind—Henry Simpson. Henry had been my coach. A self-appointed one at that. I hadn't picked him; he'd adopted me.

As a child he had polio. I guess he hadn't had a severe case—bad, but not crippling. Before cycling had much of a following in the United States, Henry rode to regain his strength. He never was a great athlete. Yet, no one I knew enjoyed the sport so much. We met at a local race and hit it off. For some unknown reason, he began teaching me everything he knew about cycling.

The success I had in races was due to his guidance. I remember the mental training he would put me through. Like Art, he stressed the importance of focus. "Focus on the one-hundred meters in front of you" was his daily challenge. He would relay story after story of losing races due to cyclists focusing on the leaders in the race too far ahead to even see. Others focused inside too much, where the pain was. He beat into my head that looking too far out in front or too closely within one's own psyche were disaster-prone scenarios. Both approaches lacked a proper focal point. It was in stringing together each one-hundred-meter segment, over the entire length of the course, where the race was won or lost.

Henry would tell me about many riders who could have won their races, but never got the chance. Why? Because they lost sight of their immediate, controllable surroundings. Loose gravel on the roadway or another rider losing control in the turn ahead caught them unprepared. The continual message he pushed was the reason they lost. They lost because they failed to focus on what was needed to win the race, that next one-hundred meters. Henry had been a real inspiration. He never took anything from me. All he did was give. I'll forever be in his debt. In fact, this reminded me I should have him over for dinner soon.

In the middle of reminiscing about Henry, it hit me. What does it take to get others to keep the right focus? A good role model. Someone to identify with. Someone like Henry was for me in cycling. And, I could say the same about Art if you were talking about business. Both of them taught me best by the example they set.

Feeling worn out from all this thinking, I let myself hear the music again. It was time to go to bed. As I turned off the music, I promised myself I wouldn't forget what I'd come up with that evening. No doubt Art and I would be having a conversation about this on Saturday.

The days leading to the weekend went by swiftly. I felt satisfied we had worked with our customers to clear up any actions on our part that were causing them concern. Having customers with high expectations was challenging yet rewarding when you came through for them. Without seeking customer feedback and acting as constant watchdogs for our own service, we could easily be lulled into complacency by our success.

Early Saturday morning I woke to see turquoise skies. This was a pleasant surprise. All week the early mornings had been gloomy with hazy afternoon sunshine being the best we could look forward to. After loading my bike on my bike rack, I sped off to Art's house a little behind schedule. The big gate was open when I arrived, which seemed strange. I had never seen it open on my arrival. Hopefully Art wasn't irritated. It was almost 8:15 a.m., and I was late.

On rounding the last turn in the driveway, I saw Art bending over his bicycle. A rag was in his right hand. It looked like he was wiping something off the frame. Still stooping, his left hand shot up in greeting. Then I noticed his bike. What a beauty. Jumping out of the car, my first words were, "Nice wheels!"

Art's face, as he straightened up, reminded me of a ten-year-old who just stepped on the plate after hitting a game-winning home run. Without the slightest attempt to hide his pride, he said, "Thanks. Today will be the shakedown cruise. I've never ridden her before. Just picked her up from the shop and can't wait to try her out."

On close inspection, I recognized the frame was a De Rosa. "Ugo De Rosa. Handmade." I petted the frame and surveyed the craftsmanship with a pang of jealousy.

"Wanta trade?" was the best I could come up with.

"Not on your life. This is the bike I'm going to ride on my first century."

Ah ha! Now I knew the reason for meeting this way. Art was training for his first one-hundred-mile bike ride. He'd done the New York Marathon and a number of triathlons. Looks like this was going to be his next big physical challenge.

"I'm happy to see you're keeping yourself so active." Trying to needle him a bit I continued, "I'm sure you'll do well. My first century was a piece of cake. However…I was much younger than you when I did it."

"That's why I have to compensate with technology. I may be older, but I'm smart enough to get all the help I can." It didn't take a psychologist to see Art didn't want to be mistaken for some old guy trying his hardest to appear young.

"How far are we going today?" I asked, trying not to appear facetious.

"I was thinking of somewhere between twenty-five and thirty miles." Then to needle me back, he said, "Unless that's too far for you…I know the demands of being a CEO probably don't allow you to keep in shape the way you used to."

We both chuckled as we mounted our bikes and started peddling. The pace was leisurely. I decided to wait for Art to start the talking. When we hit the main road, we turned right. This meant we were heading for the mountains, not down into the valley. I liked going up—less traffic. After a few minutes, Art picked up the pace slightly and started talking.

"I'm happy you joined me for my workout today, Sam. I would like you to give me some tips about how to ride. My training up till now has been pretty much solo."

Listening to Art reminded me of one of his endearing qualities. He never acted like he knew it all, even when he probably did. Nor was he too weak to ask for help. Whenever he could learn from someone, he took full advantage of the situation. If he hadn't asked me to give him some guidance, I probably wouldn't have noticed his riding at all.

I would have been more self-centered, thinking of my own agenda. In no way did I want to squander an opportunity to learn from this man.

"Sure. I'll be happy to, Art." As we started to climb, I noticed Art's posture and grip on the handlebar. "During your training, have you experienced any physical problems? Numb hands? Backache?"

After giving this some thought, Art replied, "Not much backache. Maybe a little stiffness. My real problem has been my hands. I went back to the shop where I bought the bike and they told me I needed a good pair of gloves. They've helped some. But, I'm still experiencing numbness unless I put my hands on top of the handlebar most of the time."

"Well, part of the reason could be with the way you're gripping the bar in the drops."

"The what's?" Art said, wonder in his voice.

"Sorry. Where your hands are right now, on the flat part, is what is called riding in the drops. Your hand position, near the ends, is where most inexperienced riders first learn to grip the bar. To hold the bar where you've got it adds muscle tension because your wrists are rotated downward. A better place to grip the bar is on the curved portion. Keep your wrists straight and your hands will find the right spot on the bar to grasp."

Art adjusted his grip one hand at a time. He nodded his head to show this felt more comfortable before he said, "Thanks, feels much better. I wonder why I didn't think of this myself?"

"Because you're no better or worse than most novice riders. One more tip about your grips. There are many positions you can use during a long ride. Using a number of hand positions can relieve tense muscles and prevent the numbing you're experiencing."

Over the next few miles, at Art's insistence, I described every hand variation I knew—in the drops, on the brake lever hoods, and on the tops. As we worked our way up a long, sustained climb, he asked why I was riding with my hands on the top of the bar. He wanted to know why I was in a position where I'd get more wind resistance.

"Because I'm making a tradeoff. With my upper body more vertical, I'm increasing wind resistance and making it easier to breathe. This position facilitates breathing. While climbing, the most experienced riders can grind out a better pace sitting up. It also provides a change of pace for the back, relieving tired muscles."

It didn't take Art long to change positions. Then we both fell silent for the rest of the climb to the summit. Over the crest, the terrain became rolling hills. On this part of the ride, we talked about his training regimen and how to prepare for the actual race day. From what Art already knew, he had obviously researched his goal well. We didn't talk much during this phase of the workout. Any talk was about cycling.

When we were well on our way back, I broke our silence, "I thought about what you wrote at the end of your letter."

Art looked over, "Yes?"

"I've really tried to keep things in perspective. I mean…more so than I ever have before. Focusing on what's important is a constant struggle. Just because I know I have to keep myself concentrating on the key things doesn't make everything else go away."

"Welcome to the club, Sam. Now, don't beat yourself up too much. Remember, you've been doing a great job at this your whole career. Nobody is able to stay focused a hundred percent of the time. You're better off than everyone else if you can be a percent point or two more focused than they are." As we peddled, I had to agree with him. In the last month I probably had been too hard on myself as I tried to live up to Art's advice. I wanted to be perfect.

"So you thought about the question I gave you."

"I sure did. What I came up with isn't what you'd call brilliant. More like common sense. I figured you asked me how to get others properly focused so I'd remember as CEO I can't do everything myself." As he nodded agreement, I continued, "First, I came up with the well-known, but often ignored, fact that you have to communicate clearly what it is you want people to take as important."

Art interjected, "And frequently! You have to communicate the message over and over. People forget. And priorities change. The more you talk about what's important, the more certainty you will have that others will also do what's important."

Now I was nodding agreement. Before I had a chance to say anything, Art continued, "Reminds me of an observation by Isaac Asimov. He said when you have a reputation for subtlety, it pays to be obvious. That last part relates well to what we're talking about. When it comes to helping others achieve the right focus, it pays to be obvious."

I had to agree. Picking up where I left off, I continued, "The next thing I came up with was using rewards. Give people the incentive to keep properly focused. I may be mixing things up, but I think feedback is a key part of all this. Letting people know when they are on and off track helps them maintain focus. I want people to be confident in their understanding of what the priorities are and what's important."

As I talked, Art kept nodding and I kept on speaking. "So, feedback and rewards are necessary to keep others properly focused and directed."

Hesitating slightly, I concluded, "The last thing I came up with, almost out of the blue, was having a good role model as a personal example. It makes sense to me that seeing someone else focusing on what's important is a great way to stimulate others to follow suit."

Art's nodding stopped abruptly as I finished talking. He had been nodding nonstop while I spelled out my thinking. In the ensuing silence, all I could see in reaction was the faintest crack of a smile. Or was it a frown? I couldn't really tell because he was looking straight ahead at the road.

When he finally responded, it was with a question. "What did you mean when you said your last idea came out of the blue?"

"Well, it wasn't my first idea by a long shot. I was trying to formulate a well thought-out answer to your question. The idea of serving as an example didn't come during my first pass at an answer. It popped into my head when I was thinking back to my days of competitive cycling. There was this guy, Henry. He taught me a lot technically. He also taught me about having heart—largely through example. I never knew anyone who could do as much as he could with such little talent. He really didn't have the legs for the sport. Yet, he beat out people who were much stronger."

"So, Henry was a valuable person to have around?"

"Invaluable is more like it. Without his guidance I don't think I would have amounted to anything in cycling. Not that I was of Olympic caliber. But, I had more than a taste of the thrill of victory."

"That must be the opposite of the agony of defeat my legs are feeling right now," Art mused wryly. The miles were taking their toll on his legs.

"Another thing about Henry was that he made the same point to me you did about the importance of focus. I didn't make that connection with any clarity right away. When I was digressing about Henry, I remembered he used to stress the importance of keeping focused. That's when the idea came to me about being a good example."

Art expressed genuine fascination. "I love it," he said. "It always amazes me how our creative powers often lead not to the revolutionary or new, but to the rediscovery of a simple truth. The product of our search is often something basic…the discovery of, as you said, common sense. In my estimation, you have the answer to the question of how to get others to focus on what's important."

As we headed downhill, winding through the last few miles towards Art's house, he pontificated as though he was talking to passengers in the passing cars, "'Example is not the main thing in influencing others. It is the only thing!'"

As I was about to ask who he was talking to, he interrupted with, "Albert Schweitzer…I tend to agree with him on this point. Sure, this may be a bit of an exaggeration, but Schweitzer's remark takes on more and more relevancy for those who ascend to visible positions of leadership."

'Like CEOs?' was my thought. I didn't know I had responded out loud. I thought I had only been talking to myself.

"An enlightened observation, Sam. You don't have to be in your present position as CEO to see what I'm talking about, though. Have you noticed anything different about my riding over the last twenty miles or so?"

He caught me unaware. I knew there was something specific he was looking for. But what? Nothing stood out in my mind. He didn't wait long for a reply. Art answered his own question.

"The power of example takes place in everyday life. It happens all around us, even right here. Take two people working out on bikes. I've watched when and how you've changed your hand position. Ever since you gave me that advice on placement, I've mimicked your every move. Sure, I made a slight adjustment here or there, but what I consciously decided to do was follow your lead. Whenever you changed position, I'd follow suit. It's paid off, too.

No other time after riding this long have I gone without a fair amount of numbness in my hands. They always suffer. However, right now they feel great. Thanks for being such a good example. I've learned a lot during our ride."

The old fox had set me up. This bike ride was Art's idea and his vehicle for getting his point across. I heard him loud and clear. How he could crystallize my thinking was amazing. He had a natural talent for helping me learn.

"It's always a pleasure to teach an old master like you something... anything. I have to admit you've been in that role enough times for me. If I look at how you've influenced me, I now realize how much of it has been by example. Many times I chose to handle a situation as you handled similar ones. You've been flattered countless times by my imitation."

"Good," he said, sounding pleased he'd been of help. Not wanting the conversation to degenerate into syrup, I decided to bait Art into a sprint to his house.

"Since we're on the topic of learning from example, let's see who is the role model for sprinting."

Without another word, I started to sprint. Looking back, I saw Art take the bait. For all his training and my current status as a weekend warrior, he still wasn't much of a match. I steadily pulled away. Art's property soon came into view. As I passed through the gates, I sat up and coasted until he caught up. His face had changed to vermillion. He was puffing hard.

"Guess you'll have to wait till next time to learn from the master," I gloated.

I waited for a comeback. It seemed the poor guy didn't have enough breath to answer. As we walked our bikes to the service porch door, he finally spoke, "Can I buy you a drink inside?"

"Sure." Even though part of me wanted to head home, I was happy to keep his company as long as he'd have me.

After grabbing some mineral water out of the refrigerator we went out onto the south veranda. We both stretched a little and talked about his upcoming one-hundred-mile challenge.

Reclining on a comfortable lawn chair, I swung the conversation back to what we talked about during our workout. I had been thinking about the key points Art had purposely brought to my attention, one key point per meeting.

"Is there more to the connection between focusing on what's important and what we talked about today...being a good example? I'm curious because I don't want to miss a connection if there is one. Am I missing anything?"

"Nothing of substance. You've always impressed me with your ability to absorb the essence of what I'm trying to get across. Remember, all I want to do is remind you of what you've done to deserve my trust in you. As far as I'm concerned, you haven't learned a thing from me during our last two meetings. You've been focusing on what's important. You already make an excellent example for others. All I want to do is make you more aware of these actions. Why? Because, as a leader, you are going to need these skills more than ever."

After a pause he continued, "I'm glad you're taking our talks so seriously. Your ability to lead by example and keep the proper focus has prepared you for leading your organization. Now you have to do both these things even better. Whether you believe it or not, you've achieved a kind of celebrity status. Reaching such a status means people watch your every move. Lots of them. As CEO, you have enormous visibility."

"Sounds kind of ominous," was my retort.

"Yes, it can be. It's also an opportunity to make a bigger impact doing the same things you've done before achieving your present stature. You see, focusing on what's important and leading by example is intertwined. If you do both, you are consistent and don't create any dissonance…know what I mean?"

"If there is only one person leading by example and focusing on what's important in the organization, I can see it better be me. But, isn't my job to get everyone else involved?"

"That's right. The more others act as positive examples, the easier your job becomes."

In the back of my mind I began to question how to lead by example in order to keep others properly focused. I tried to think back to what Art had done when he was in the role. One thing immediately came to mind—the questions he always asked. We had talked about that in our conversation last month. I remember he had developed a set of specific questions to keep himself and others on track. This was one of the most important things I had learned from our conversations.

"Last month when we met for dinner, you talked about using questions to keep me, as well as yourself, moving down the right path. If my memory's correct, you said you tried to ask yourself each morning, *What do I have to do today to focus on what's important?* Then, during the day as you got caught up in the fray of things, you'd ask, *Is this really worth doing?* When you ask those questions of others, you'd be signaling them to think in a similar fashion. At least that's how I took it."

"Yes. One of the best ways to be an example to others is having what I call a sound questioning routine. People know what's important to you by the questions you ask. If all you ever ask is *How are profits, or the bottom line?* what do you think people would say is important to you? And, if all you ever ask is, *How are our customer satisfaction numbers?* what would they say? Smart managers continually ask the questions that relate to what they want others to focus on. Do you remember the set of questions I told you I disciplined myself to ask whenever I had an important decision to make?"

Knowing he didn't expect an instant answer, I took a minute to search my memory. In Art's study that night, I had asked how he was able to keep himself focusing on what's important. He rattled off a set of questions. I remember I'd wished I could have taken notes. What were those questions?

Trying to buy time, I pointed to my tongue and said, "They're on the tip of my tongue." Art sat patiently. He didn't seem in any hurry.

The mental wall between my memory and my recall seemed to rise the harder I tried. So I took another tack. I gave up. Before conceding defeat, however, I decided to come up with my own list. Art had been saying I knew all the answers already.

I might as well prove him right. What are the simple, obvious things we have to do to be successful? The first that came to mind was the customer. The rest fell into place.

In my exuberance, I didn't even allow myself to walk through my list of questions before responding. They just flowed out, "The questions I would ask are: Does this help the customer? Does this help our people? Does this help our company and values? Does this help..." Then I got stuck. "Does this help...I know there's more....Damn it, I can't get it. Help, will you, Art?"

"My pleasure. The only thing you left off my list was results. This is different from the people whose job it is to achieve those results. My internal questioning routine goes: Does this help our customers? Results? People? Our organization? Our values?

Keeping these commitments creates a reinforcing cycle. The company provides for our people. They, in turn, are dedicated to achieving results that serve our customers. Satisfied customers close the loop by supporting our company. The glue holding all this together is our values. It's that simple. Yet, it takes a lot of persistence and focus to make sure that positive cycle doesn't break down somewhere."

Feeling like I didn't want to lose any of this again, I asked for a piece of paper. Art chuckled and said, "Sure. We can get some in the study."

Once back in his study, Art found the scratch pad he had written on last time. On it he wrote *focus on what's important* and underneath, *lead by example.* He gave me a legal note pad from a drawer, a pen, and this piece of paper. As I wrote down the questions we had talked about outside, Art waited patiently.

"How about lunch?" he interjected just as I finished.

Sounded good after our workout. While Art checked with Marilyn, I called home. Kris rounded up the kids while I drove home and showered. We met at Mort's, a local deli in town. My kids liked Art and Marilyn a lot.

Where Marilyn was living proof of the power of human kindness, Art showed he hadn't forgotten what it was like to be a kid. He related to our teenagers on their terms. Like many twelve- and fifteen-year-olds, mine were usually quiet around adults. Today was different. We all had a great lunch together.

Later that night, I replayed what we had discussed earlier in the day. I realized no one escapes from leading by example. The only question is, what example are we setting? Is it the one we really want, or do our actions reflect what really isn't all that important? That night I slept like a rock. I don't know if it was because of the mental calisthenics Art put me through, or that killer bike ride.

*We can't all be heroes, because somebody has
to sit on the curb and clap as they go by.*

— Will Rogers

Chapter 4

REWARD SUCCESS

November was going to be my month to take the initiative. Before Art had a chance to pick a time and place to meet, I wrote inviting him to the Hollywood Bowl. A tradition had started in our company many years ago. We took over the Bowl during the off-season for a night of celebration. Art had started the annual party ten years ago. This year would be the first celebration without him unless I persuaded him to come.

As I expected, he called regarding the invitation. Art was always sensitive to my needs. He wanted this event to be seen as the company's, not tied to him. Knowing he would question the invitation, I was prepared. I reminded him that this event was, by design, a pure celebration. No one was singled out during the evening. The next objection he raised was the rule about no retirees. He reminded me of the importance of keeping this an employee and family event. No customers, vendors, or outside guests were ever allowed.

Because he was not giving in easily I decided to play hardball. I knew he'd have difficulty with the question, "How many current employees consider you no longer a member of our family?" When I asked the question, he knew he could forget bowing out. Art was too smart to fight a battle he knew he would lose. Before graciously agreeing to go, however, he toyed with me. He was not willing to show defeat too easily.

The last thing he said struck me. He said our meeting at the yearly gathering at the Bowl was really "most apropos." As usual, I knew he had something up his sleeve. But, this time, so did I.

The beauty of the Hollywood Bowl celebration lies in its intent. The night belongs to the people in the organization. There are no long speeches. Everyone is treated to the same evening of superb food and entertainment. Even though it is clearly a recognition event for what we had accomplished together over the last fiscal year, the agenda stays simple. There is only one goal—have fun.

Every department in the company selects those who contributed to the department's success and best exemplified our values over the last twelve months. Those selected are seated in the box seats near the front of the stage. The only restriction to these departmental decisions is that no managers can be picked. Managers are handled differently. A special executive committee picks a handful of managers on the same criteria used by the departments. This is the only gesture towards individual recognition. For the selectees, it is considered a real honor to sit in one of the boxes. Everyone else sits in the bleachers behind the box seats.

Art always sat in the upper reaches of the nosebleed section when he ran the company. At the end of the evening, he would stroll down to the stage and sum up the evening. He never spoke for more than two to four minutes. The evening was ninety-nine percent food, fun, and entertainment. Only one percent was company-related. To my knowledge, no one ever complained of a bad time. In fact it was just the opposite. People always talked about how great they felt about the annual night at the Bowl.

Probably the most difficult task leading up to the evening is picking the right entertainment. The evening always starts with a performance by the Philharmonic. The first half of the show traditionally is classical music. Then the pace changes in the second half to more contemporary music.

What always made each of these performances special was the preparation. Many times the songs and the artist's off-handed remarks were tailored to fit our situation. No one knew who was going to play until the performer or performers walked on stage after intermission. Part of the fun was trying to guess who had been lined up for the evening.

Tonight we had signed Frontier Theory. For the first time I was the one who had the ultimate responsibility for the choice. The committee making the final recommendation knew I planned to have Art in the audience. They did their homework and discovered this Washington DC band fit Art's taste in music. Even better, they fit perfectly with my agenda.

Frontier Theory is made up of four young brothers, each pursuing a different professional career. They work as a band part-time. Even so, their music is good enough to have won awards. The committee had done an outstanding job working with the Philharmonic and Frontier Theory to put together a wonderful show.

Still, with the added burden of being in charge, I wondered if the evening was going to be as enjoyable as it had been in the past. Right at this moment I felt a special appreciation for all Art had done. He made sure very few people were burdened with preparations for the event. His goal was to have as many as possible enjoy themselves as guests. That was why I wanted him at the Bowl. I had a real surprise for him.

We had arranged for me to pick up Art at his country club. Before my invitation to the Bowl, Art had invited some of the staff from the local chapter of the Red Cross to play golf. Kris and the kids were going to pick up Marilyn at home and meet us there. Art was waiting in the parking lot as I pulled up front.

"Great weather," he said and then added, "I'm sure you're relieved about that."

He was right about the weather. November can be an iffy month. It's rarely too cold. But, it can rain. The forecast for tonight was clear skies, lows in the upper 50s, and a trace of wind. Couldn't be better. Unless, of course, a warm Santa Ana was blowing. Then it would be like a summer's night.

I wiped my brow, removing imaginary beads of sweat. "Thank God for small miracles. Every night last week I dreamed I was fighting hurricanes, snow storms, or monsoons. Nothing pleases me more than seeing *el sol* shining over yonder."

As we headed east towards Hollywood, the sun behind us was dropping low on the horizon. We were to arrive early enough to help with last-minute details. Art had always worked during dinner, serving food. I planned to keep this tradition going. I wanted him to finally get a chance to sit down for dinner.

However I figured he'd rather roll up his sleeves and do what he'd always done. I was sure he was going to volunteer to work. Whether or not to let him puzzled me. On the one hand, I should let him do it. He always had a great time being a waiter. On the other hand, he deserved the opportunity to sit with his old employees and enjoy himself.

I relished the vision of a bunch of employees carrying him away, kicking and screaming, to dine with some lucky table of admirers. He interrupted this pleasurable thought by asking, "What do you plan on doing when we get there?"

Trying not to slip up, I responded, "Same as you always did. I plan on serving food." Then, to test the waters, I dangled, "Gee, I wonder what we ought to do with you?"

Smiling, he took the bait, "Maybe I'll just mingle during dinner. Now that I'm officially retired, it's time for me to try something new. No more waiting on tables for those measly tips. If you don't mind, I'll fend for myself while you work. It'll be fun seeing everyone again."

That was easy, I thought. The only negative part of this quick resolution was not having the chance to visualize Art being manhandled by a crowd of merry pranksters. Still, he might suffer that fate anyway. As soon as we arrived, I knew everyone who saw him would stampede to greet him. People's fondness toward Art hadn't changed one bit.

Approaching the Bowl, I thought how good tonight would be for him. No doubt he misses being part of the action. It will also be great for the organization. While parking the car, my apprehension began to rise. I certainly wanted everything to go as scheduled. The success of this event must be upheld.

Waiting, trying not to look too conspicuous, were a few well-chosen employees who knew Art would be arriving in my car. Most of them were on the entertainment committee.

Virtually no one else knew he was coming. I wanted genuine surprise and spontaneity to mark the evening. A good actor friend always used a line he had stolen. "My spontaneity is well-rehearsed." I definitely didn't want to give people a chance to rehearse what they were going to say when they saw Art. Only a few of my committee members needed rehearsal. The rest of the plan would take care of itself.

As we walked towards the front entrance, the ambush went off without a hint of a setup. So far, success. Art was whisked off, as he said, to mingle. I went to don an apron and check in to see if I was needed anywhere. Years of conducting this affair with Aliments, a truly professional caterer, certainly had its benefits. Apparently this well-oiled machine was motoring along with its usual efficiency.

The guests are asked to arrive between six and seven o'clock. Most arrive about five forty-five. Being fashionably late has never applied to this evening. If anything, people complain the night doesn't last long enough. So they arrive as early as they dare. I've always equated this event with Disneyland—the only other place I've ever gone where everyone is smiling. The atmosphere is contagious. You can close your eyes in the crowd and feel the "good times" around you.

For the dinner portion of the evening, the honored employees in the box seats are fed where they sit. Everyone else eats in the areas immediately adjacent to the Bowl itself. In order to feed everyone comfortably, the rest of the property becomes one big restaurant. The lighting and the table decorations create a serpentine effect through the nooks and crannies winding through the property, giving the area surrounding the Bowl a different perspective. It's a spectacular display of light and merriment.

As Art had always done, I served in the box seats. Dinner slipped by too fast. As I saw people beginning to filter into their seats above us, I panicked. Had people been rushed through dinner? Thankfully, when I looked at my watch, I realized dinner had begun over an hour and a half ago. The people I was serving were probably a little slower than the rest because they didn't have to navigate from the tables to their seats for the performance.

The Philharmonic started promptly at eight thirty with the music of Mozart. For the younger part of the audience, Amadeus was a more recognizable name, given the success of the movie. I met Art at his accustomed seat a couple of rows from the top. It was easy to see why Art liked this position. You could look down and see the Bowl filled with almost four thousand employees of the company with their families. As I nestled into a seat between my two kids, I feigned breathlessness and leaned over to ask Art, "Why didn't you pick the last row?"

"Sam, I've never sat in the last row. It doesn't give the wonderful feeling of being surrounded. I always liked having coworkers sitting on all sides. Funny thing is, even though it's a new group every year, they seem to act like it's a bigger honor to be behind me than to sit up front. Those rascals in the last two rows always seem to be having the most fun."

I didn't comment on why this was true. I knew the answer. Everyone loved this guy. They loved being around him. If the nosebleed section was good enough for Art, it was good enough for them. With such strong identification, people naturally chose to be like him. The reality was, no one picked where they sat except Art. Each department rotated through the various sections. Some years they were in front. Others, near the back. A systems guy had figured out the rotation scheme. We've never had to adjust it because it just works.

During the show I knew Art and I wouldn't have a chance to talk. Etiquette in the Bowl excluded talking during performances. At intermission, Art would be confronted with a steady stream of well-wishers ascending on us from every direction. As far as I was concerned, this was fine. Let him be the center of attention. I was using the time to mentally prepare for the surprise I had for him.

The show started with the overture to *The Magic Flute*, Mozart's final opera. We committee members felt this was an especially appropriate opening. Knowing Art would be in attendance, we saw parallels between this piece and the end of Art's active involvement in the company. Even more significantly, Mozart composed this last piece as a vehicle to symbolize some of his most deeply held beliefs about Freemasonry. He was a man convinced that striving for self-improvement and facing ordeals were necessary to reach the goal of true humanity and become part of the brotherhood of men. Though not a Freemason, Art, like Mozart, was a man holding dearly to a set of basic beliefs.

Intermission went just as I thought. The lines waiting to see Art were longer than the lines for the women's bathroom. When the show resumed, Frontier Theory's performance was magnificent. Not only was their music superb, but it was also their warmth and good humor that infected the crowd. With the start of the final number, I excused myself and took the side entrance.

I made my way quickly down the hill to the rear of the stage. The dying applause after the second curtain call was my cue to walk on stage. I headed directly for the podium. This was the second time I had seen things from this vantage point. The first was my rehearsal yesterday. Then the stands were empty. Now, with thousands of faces sweeping up the horizon, the pit in my stomach felt like a pumpkin was ripening in there.

I told myself not to start with the *I'll be brief* routine. To most people, this signals that the speaker will be anything *but* brief. Instead, I figured to let my brevity speak for itself. I wanted to keep within five minutes.

"Thank you all for coming tonight. I trust you've enjoyed the show as much as I have." As applause rolled around the amphitheater, I paused before proceeding.

"Tonight I want to keep the tradition of this evening alive and well. If we've succeeded, this evening has been just like every November we have celebrated together here at the Bowl. For all the contributions you have made to our business success, for all the praises sung to us from our customers and vendors, for all the glitter and glory bestowed on us by Wall Street, you are the ones who deserve the credit.

Tonight is a small, but hopefully lasting token of appreciation for the success you have brought the company. In a world of change, this celebration of our victories—and the memories we take from it—should be a constant. I want all of us to maintain this tradition."

Pausing for emphasis, I continued, "Yet, speaking to you about tradition…I also want to break with it. When I think about credit due, when I review the reasons for our success, there is one thing I want to do tonight that breaks with the past. I want to single out someone for special recognition.

Certainly our purpose here is recognizing what we have all done together. I know that. Yet, we have a unique opportunity this evening. I'd be surprised if anyone doesn't know what that opportunity is; and, who I want to publicly recognize. Yes, I think most of you have seen him here tonight: Art Brunsing."

A smile formed on my face as I pretended to scan the horizon for Art's whereabouts.

"Art, I know you're squirming in your seat and probably not real happy I'm doing this. Well, just squirm some more." Then I asked the audience, "Are we happy Art joined us tonight?"

The reaction was pandemonium. People clapped. People whistled. People screamed. The sound was deafening. As his ovation continued, a powerful feeling came over me. I felt proud of these people. I was proud of their love for this man. I was warmed by their understanding of what he had built.

After a minute of unrelenting cheering I began hushing the crowd. "Please…Please…," I kept saying, "Please, I'm not finished."

When the noise dropped to a reasonable level, I continued. "Art, for all you have done for us that will last forever in our most cherished memories, we want to give something back. Knowing of your love and belief in young people, the board of directors has approved the start-up of a foundation. The sole purpose of this foundation is to provide academic scholarships for college."

Holding up a mock scholarship, I explained the details,

"The Arthur W. Brunsing Scholarship Fund will meet the full financial need of each recipient. I do not want to get into the particulars here. What I would like to do is tell you about the uniqueness of these scholarships. If we are going to name something after you, Art, we decided it should resemble you.

So, we decided to be creative and different from other scholarship programs. These scholarships will be awarded to students the summer before they start their senior year of high school. The scholarship will pay all tuition, room and board, and incidentals over four full years at whatever school the recipient winds up attending. Recipients can get an early start on making their dreams a reality.

With the scholarship in their pockets, they have more options during their senior year. If they never thought of a Harvard or Stanford as a viable option, now they can. Maybe they will try harder to get into a better school. When they win the scholarship, there's no dollar amount specified. We'll pay for wherever they go. It could be a reasonably priced state university program the student is looking for. Or, it could be a high-priced private school. The choice is up to them. We just pick up the tab. Kind of what you've done for many of us, Art."

Pretending to hold up a pair of imaginary binoculars to my eyes, I said, "I can't see you way up there in the back. Let me say in closing, it has been a rare honor to work with you. The board is thrilled with the opportunity to create this foundation as a way to perpetuate your memory. Thanks a million."

Before I could say good night, the crowd rose to its feet and gave the loudest ovation of the evening. There was nothing for me to do but join in the tribute. Soon a chant began to rise, Speech…Speech…Speech… Speech. As I looked toward where Art was sitting, I saw what appeared to be the start of a procession.

This cavalcade descended the center aisle with Art being escorted by a woman on either side. One of them was Marcie. She had been his secretary for years before I was fortunate enough to inherit her. The other woman was a fun-loving and boisterous manager from the West Coast Customer Support Center.

Art seemed a reluctant victim as they marched, stride for stride, down the steps. The top rows were filing down after them leaving a bald spot created by the empty bleachers. The cadence of the salvos matched Art's footsteps. There was no let up on enthusiasm until Art reached the podium.

I stepped back out of his spotlight. He tried to wave me back to the podium, but I wouldn't budge. Once Art was on stage, the cheering erupted again into another round of pandemonium. He was using his best body language to shut them all up. I was relishing the moment. My plan had worked. Art was getting a taste of his just reward. And, the employees were going nuts.

No one sat down as the cheering subsided. The aisles were full. Everyone wanted to get closer. Art couldn't hide how moved he was. His eyes were full of tears. A blinding smile spanned his features. Hands folded over his heart, he stood silently searching for words to say. Finally, he spoke.

"Let me share a secret with you, my friends. A secret I've shared with only a handful of people. One of my lifelong fantasies was to be a rock star. To be up on stage with a packed house. To hear the thunderous applause. Well, tonight you've made an old man feel like a rock star... maybe better. Thank you."

He stepped back from the microphone and waved a kiss to the throng of admirers. Nobody moved. Another thunderous hurrah broke out. The audience wanted to top the decibel reading of all previous ovations. They wanted him back at the podium. He wouldn't oblige. They persisted. He reluctantly approached to within two feet of the microphone and yelled in a couple of thank-yous before leaving the stage.

I followed him. For all the planning I had done, I never really thought about this juncture of the evening. Since I was his ride home, I figured we better stick together. When I caught up with him, Art seemed flustered. Embarrassed was probably more accurate.

He said, "I don't know if I'm coming or going, whether I should stick around or leave." I suggested we head for the car. Art said, "No, actually I'd like to go for a walk. Are we blocking anybody with your car?"

The car was parked in a spot that wouldn't pin anyone in. Art led me to the picnic area across Highland Boulevard. We sat on top of a picnic table. Facing the Bowl, we watched the people trickle to their cars and the cars flow down the street.

"I can't tell you how much I appreciate what you did for me tonight."

"You're welcome. I'm just glad you came. I had my doubts I was gonna convince you."

"I know," Art conceded. "The reason I was so hesitant was I had a pretty good idea what you were up to. I figured you'd somehow get me on stage. That kind of thing always embarrasses me. Whether you know it or not, I get embarrassed easily."

"Are you trying to tell me you didn't enjoy the attention?"

"Not at all. I wouldn't change a thing. I loved it…now that it's over. Beforehand was when the whole thing seemed a lot more uncomfortable. For me, it's so much easier to give recognition than take it. That's why I played hard to get."

As he talked, all I could think about was how happy I was to be the one to tell him about the foundation dedicated in his name.

"Well, this time the pleasure was all mine. You being the one recognized was a welcome change. You've always been so good about spreading accolades and glory to everyone else."

While I was talking, Art reached into his pocket and pulled something out. I noticed it was a piece of paper from the note pad in his study.

"Do you remember what I said when I finally agreed to come to the celebration tonight?" I didn't.

This must have been obvious because Art didn't wait for my answer. "I said coming tonight would be very apropos."

Tapping the paper in his hand, he added, "What do you think I wrote on the paper for tonight?"

In all my excitement about surprising Art, I never considered what we might talk about tonight. What would be appropriate? Probably something to do with recognition. What would be a catchy phrase that would capture the essence of this evening? *Celebrate the victories* came to mind. So I proposed my first reaction, "How about celebrate the victories?"

He seemed pleased with my answer.

"Perfect. Maybe even a better way of saying it than what I wrote." He then handed me the paper. On it was written *Focus on what's important, Lead by example,* and *Reward success.* Art studied my face, following my eyes as I scanned the page.

At the moment I finished reading *Reward success,* he interjected, "What's the fundamental purpose of bringing everyone to the Hollywood Bowl? To reward success. It is essential to tangibly show people we care about their accomplishments.

Using your way of putting it, Sam, we have to let people know we believe the victories they have brought us are worth celebrating. It's so easy to be seduced into next year's challenges without first rewarding ourselves for what we've just achieved. We are fortunate to have such a dedicated and talented work force. Every year since our first celebration, we have met our stretch goals. What would you do if we didn't make our targets? If we had a bad year? It can happen, you know."

Looking down at *reward success,* the answer seemed blatantly obvious.

"Our job is to reward success, not failure. I'd forego the night at the Bowl…and work like a dog to ensure we only went one year without the glory."

Art nodded agreement. "Yes, recognition is a powerful tool. Yet, it only works for you if it's deserved. Otherwise it's meaningless flattery, benefiting no one."

My mind was racing ahead of what Art was saying. Or, maybe it was racing backwards, making associations. I thought about the first time I was selected to sit in the box seats as a manager. The feeling was easy to remember. It felt wonderful. I had enjoyed a most successful year. The honor of being selected was especially rewarding after all that hard work. The evening at the Hollywood Bowl had provided a positive sense of closure to me. After that night, I felt ready to take on the challenges I knew were in store for us in the upcoming year.

Then my thoughts returned to tonight. I saw, as if it was happening again, my own actions on stage. This time I could see myself from the outside. I knew how I had felt. Now I was seeing it.

When they were bringing Art down the center aisle, the smile on my face rivaled the Cheshire Cat's. My God, I was enjoying myself. What Art said was true. It can be more satisfying, and easier, to give recognition than get it. I wanted to talk about this.

"The way I see it, recognition is certainly one of the most important things we do. I can see that more clearly when I think about you. Tonight was really different. I know you've received many awards and honors over the years, but not from your own organization. You've always been the one giving out all the honors and awards.

Tonight was probably the first time most of our employees saw you get any tangible recognition. I remember the last time we met; we talked about the importance of setting the example for others. You have been the best example I know of giving credit rather than taking it. I always admired that about you. It's had a lasting impression on me."

"That's nice of you to say, Sam. As managers, our job is to give credit, not take it for ourselves. For many who like to think of themselves as managers, this is one of the hardest lessons to learn. I appreciate your feedback that I've done a good job. Heaven knows I've tried to reward others for their success."

Try? He made it look effortless. Besides the Hollywood Bowl celebration, our organization offers all kinds of incentives for performance. Everyone is part of the profit-sharing pool. A certain percentage of compensation is tied to individual performance. We pay for profit-creating ideas. New incentive schemes are constantly being implemented. The bottom line for this organization is that we spread the wealth around. The more we spread, the bigger the pie seems to get. My own feeling about Art is he never appeared to be greedy.

"Art, you've been on the generous side of rewarding success...and that's probably an understatement. What influenced you to reward success the way you have?"

"Excellent question, Sam. Let me try to sort it out for you. I guess what I think about first is human nature. One thing we know about human beings, they are the most adaptable creatures on earth. One area where we are remarkably adaptable is with reward systems. When thrust into a new situation, people will quickly learn what's rewarded. From that point on, they will use this knowledge to their best advantage."

I interjected, "People do what they think gets rewarded."

"Well put. I never forgot a wonderful article written years ago. It was called *The Folly of Hoping for A While Rewarding B*. I don't remember the author's name. But I do remember the point. The point is, it's not what you wish people to do that matters. It's what gets rewarded. If you want performance, you have to reward performance. If you want quality, reward quality. If you want teamwork, reward teamwork.

What I learned over the years is when you give people rewards, make sure they make the connection you want them to make. Make sure they see they were rewarded for what you wanted them to do. The goal is to ritualize what you want people to do."

"What do you mean ritualize?"

"Ritualizing imprints a memory of the experience. Dramatizing and ritualizing events help intensify the experience and the resulting impact. Rewards close the loop on someone's experience."

"I get it. Sort of a rite of passage that helps employees put the past behind them and move on to the future."

"Yes. And, it also makes past experiences more positive, meaningful, and real for people."

Art's logic made me think about tonight as a reward. Did everyone make the right connections? I wanted people to connect this event to the overall achievement of company goals for the past year. By inviting every person in the organization, I hoped the message would ring out loud and clear. We all contributed in our own way to the bottom line.

I wonder how strong this message really was? Did people link the importance of teamwork to our success? No matter how well we think we reward individual contribution, there are going to be countless contributors who go unnoticed. Tonight was a night to make up for some of that. It's everyone's night.

"Art, do you think people made the right associations tonight?"

"Not everyone. Some are probably cynical about it. Looking at the big picture though, I think the vast majority felt rewarded. Also, they are leaving with a sense of closure on the past and a renewed vigor for the future."

Looking me right in the eye, he said, "You will never please everyone when it comes to rewards. You are playing a numbers game. Tonight you did great, Sam."

"Thanks for the compliment. I guess I just want to hit 100 percent."

"Let me speak just for Art Brunsing then. You captured something special with the recognition you gave me tonight. The scholarship program was truly unexpected. I couldn't be more pleased with what you and the board did. The way it's set up is very personal. The best rewards are tailored to individual needs.

You know I love young people. You know I like to be a little bit different. Anything with my stamp on it has to have a touch of novelty. Out of all the recognition I've ever received, I'll treasure this as one of the most meaningful. Thank you again."

I could feel my face flush with the rush of blood to my cheeks. Art's praise embarrassed me. I'd also take this kind of embarrassment any time. I knew these words were linked to a sincerity as solid as bedrock. Sensing my discomfort, he gave me a hearty slap on the back and nodded for us to call it a night.

Seeing the car alone in the parking lot made me realize how cool the night had become. Still, it was a warm walk back.

The most insidious disease in business is complacency.
I call it psychosclerosis: a hardening of the attitudes.

— F.G. "Buck" Rodgers

Chapter 5

MANAGE DISRESPECT

Earlier today I called Art. Our original plan was to meet for dinner next week. I didn't want to wait. When I called him this morning, I would have been willing to hop in the car and drive right over to his house. Unfortunately Art had a prior commitment, so this was not possible. He was attending a function at the old J. Paul Getty Museum at the western edge of Pacific Palisades. Given my sense of urgency, he suggested we meet at two thirty on the bluffs above the Getty.

It was now two twenty. I'd already been sitting here for fifteen minutes. Being early didn't stop me from considering the possibility I was waiting in the wrong spot. It didn't matter that my worry had no solid foundation. Art had been very specific with his directions.

From the spot we were to meet, no houses obstructed the view. This was one of maybe two spots in the area that fit that requirement. He also gave me one key landmark to look for—a tall, stately Eucalyptus growing right on the edge of the bluff.

As I stared at this tree, I failed to notice a figure walking up behind my car. The knock on the window came unexpectedly. Whisking around, I caught Art's smiling face. My first instinct was to knock his block off.

I wasn't used to getting startled like that. My second instinct was to laugh at myself. I'm sure he had no intention of sneaking up on me. It wasn't his fault I was too preoccupied to notice his arrival.

Rolling down the window, I said, "Boy, you really gave me a start!"

"Sorry," he apologized. "Let's go over and sit on the railing."

He motioned to the thick, white guardrail running along the roadway next to the bluff. The area around us was rather unstable geologically. Earthquakes, mudslides, and erosion had eaten away the bluffs. Situated about 200 feet above the Coast Highway, the view looked more south than west across Santa Monica Bay.

The December breeze off the water was nippy, almost biting. I buttoned my coat on the way to our perch above the Pacific. Before sitting, Art asked, "What's on your mind? You sounded rather concerned when you called."

He was right about my state of mind. One of the agenda items on my staff meeting this morning was a review of our social programs, especially the Special Olympics. I had not expected the reaction I got from my staff. Instead of a positive response, what I got was a strong protest. A mounting coalition had tried to axe the whole idea of associating with Special Olympics.

"Art, you know as well as I do, we've had a long-standing relationship with the Special Olympics program in California. I was surprised a number of my staff voiced strong resistance to contributing to the program this year. They felt we have been concentrating too much support on that cause. The cost of the company's involvement, I have to admit, was significant. A suggestion was raised to cut this program from our list of charitable causes. When I asked if the suggestion was for this year only, the answer was an emphatic 'no'. They felt the cut should be permanent."

Art took in what I said and then asked, "Obviously you've given this some thought. What do you think of their suggestion?"

"As you might guess, I'm torn. That's why I wanted to talk with you. On the one hand, I see the value of saving money. And, I only want this program if the time and funds we donate genuinely have a payback to those kids. If not, I'd axe the program myself. On the other hand, I'm willing to spend the money if it helps, and our employees are still committed to this cause."

"Before you encountered resistance today, what were your feelings toward our involvement?"

This wasn't hard to answer. "Honestly, before the meeting I felt this was a nonissue, a rubber stamp item. There never was resistance to this idea before. I've always been a strong supporter myself. I guess I was wrong in thinking everyone else was, too."

"Why have you been a supporter, Sam?"

I had been asking myself this very question over and over all morning. "I feel the program is well designed. The feature I especially like about it is the hands on nature of our involvement. I think the experience of working with the kids enriches us all. And, the majority of employees who have been involved seem really touched by the experience."

"Okay. You basically like the program. Now it seems all you have to do is determine how the rank and file perceives the program. This is only my opinion and it's largely an assumption, but I'd guess the program is still living up to its original purpose. For me, the satisfaction of being directly involved has not diminished over the years. Not having been there, I'm having a difficult time understanding what happened in your meeting to make this a tough decision. So far, it sounds like you have no reason to axe the program."

"What surprised me most was the force with which a couple of people presented their opposition. They were really fired up. I found myself squarely on the defensive. Without anticipating any dissension, I felt inarticulate while answering their objections. After some heated exchanges, I bought time by saying I'd give this careful thought. I told them I'd get back to them as quickly as I could."

"Smart move, Sam. I assume that's when you called me. Now, getting back to this morning's meeting, what were the major objections raised?"

I reconstructed each of the objections as best I could, trying to phrase them just as they were presented to me in the meeting. Art listened attentively, without interruption. As I strung together each opposing point, I found myself surprisingly unimpressed with their substance. The rationale behind each objection didn't seem too difficult to refute here on the bluff. Even though it's always easier to deal with a situation from hindsight, I must have been swayed quite heavily by the strength of my dissenters' conviction.

When I finished, he didn't say anything. He simply stared out to sea. I knew the wheels were turning. I waited patiently, joining him in gazing out toward the horizon. When he finally spoke, he said, "May I guess who raised these objections?"

As I nodded approval, he continued. "Curt Freeman and Patty Simpson took the lead...am I right?"

He knew he was right. Even though a few others sided with them, Curt and Patty had talked most of the time. Curt had been the one who first levied an objection, almost as soon as I brought up the subject.

"You have to be careful here, Sam. Curt is a bright individual. Besides good preparation, he will pick his time and place to influence you and the group. I picked him for his job because of those skills. He serves the company in a critical area. As far as I'm concerned, there is just one thing you have to manage with Curt. Can you guess what that is?"

My first inclination was to search for evidence of how I'd seen Art deal with Curt. Overall, he seemed to give Curt room to maneuver in his job. As chief financial officer, Curt's viewpoint was incorporated in almost every major decision. In our meetings, Art always asked for and listened to his input. Following that line of reasoning, I should carefully listen to Curt's input, too. But, this didn't make much sense here.

"What is it I need to manage with Curt?" I said rhetorically.

"Good question, Art. Based on my recollection of how you managed Curt, I'm not coming up with any clear-cut answers. You certainly trusted him a lot as chief financial officer. His viewpoint carried a lot of weight in decision-making. Your management approach with him was largely one of participation in meetings and delegation in his area of responsibility. I'm searching for a clue in your approach to dealing with him."

"Look less at my behavior when you've seen us together in public. Look more at what you know about Curt himself. Curt has a long list of strengths. You've already addressed those when you mentioned my overall approach of participation and delegation. What is much more relevant is his weaknesses. What might those be?"

Thinking about Curt, my only real reservation about him was that he tends to be too negative and a complainer. If there is a down side, he'll find it. He's also about as stubborn as they come. Now being stubborn isn't all bad. It's just that Curt can be quite sarcastic while he's at it.

"If there's anything about Curt I'd like to see change, it would be his negativism. He usually comes up with all the reasons not to do something instead of any positive reasons why we should. I need him to be a professional skeptic in CFO role. I don't need him to act so negative."

Art didn't seem to agree with my statement when he said, "Don't be too hasty about changing those things in Curt. Sometime we'll talk more about Curt's tendencies to play the devil's advocate. Is it really his skepticism that bothers you?"

No, it wasn't. It was more his approach.

"When I think about it, I guess not. It's more his sharp tongue. He can be so caustic and unconstructive. Take this morning. When he'd make a point, he'd overemphasize it with phrases like, 'We're not here to run a charity'; 'While we're at it, why not pass out Christmas turkeys'; and the one that hit me the hardest, 'We're being taken; they're laughing all the way to the bank.' He's just a bit too cynical for my liking."

"Or mine," Art added. "This is the same weakness I've seen in Curt. Have you given much thought as to how you would manage this behavior?"

Once again, my first instinct was to put Art into the role and picture how he'd handle the situation. I couldn't really recall any time Art dealt with Curt's cynicism in my presence. That was a clue. Probably dealing with Curt at the meeting this morning would have been the wrong time and the wrong place. Anyway, this is an issue I'd rather handle in private. Nonetheless, Curt needs to be confronted. I was beginning to see what was really causing me concern.

"Thanks, Art. I think I see what's been bothering me and it's not what I thought it was. The Special Olympics sponsorship isn't the problem. We aren't giving anything away. The program is working just fine. No one's taking advantage of us. What's really on my mind is Curt. I'm afraid he's trying to undermine a good program. Sure, he's entitled to his opinion. And, I want him to disagree when he needs to."

"I wholeheartedly agree."

"What I don't want him to do is let his cynical, sarcastic comments affect others. It's time I confront Curt about my dissatisfaction with his behavior. I can't blame him or expect him to stop his sarcastic remarks without leveling with him. I'll talk to him tomorrow in private."

"Again, I agree," Art enthusiastically replied. "Curt needs to learn from you what you expect. I had my own chats with him on this subject. My goal was never to change him, just to manage his tendency for using sarcasm to push his viewpoint. You have to recognize he learned to use a cynical tongue long before you or I ever met him."

"So what did you do?"

"From me he learned what was acceptable behavior and what was not. Disparaging remarks were off limits on company time. He was warned not to make them public. If he couldn't help himself, he was allowed to vent in my office. Behind closed doors, he could say anything he wanted to me. And, let me tell you, he took full advantage of my offer...Many times...Curt is an extremely valuable person. I'd personally put up with his sarcastic nature before losing him. He's strong-headed enough to quit if I pushed him too hard on this. The understanding we reached was he was not to spread cynicism anywhere inside the company."

During Art's explanation of how he'd dealt with Curt, I speculated at how difficult it must have been for Curt to keep the muzzle on. I really can't remember Curt acting as sarcastic as he had this morning when Art was running things. For years he'd kept himself under control. I also realized Curt made remarks that were awfully cynical when it was just him and me together. Say, when just the two of us were in his office.

I thought about startling Art a little bit, like he did when he knocked on my car window, by saying, "You know, I just realized something. On one level you just admitted failure to me. When you asked me about Curt's weaknesses, I came up with cynicism. You just said your goal was to manage his cynicism. Since I was able to see this weakness in Curt, you didn't fully succeed."

Art looked like he was going to speak. I wanted to finish before he had a chance to reply. So, I put out my hand signaling I wasn't finished.

"As I said, it looks like you didn't succeed very well with Curt...Yet I appreciate the fact you had a big impact on him. On another level, I think one could say you succeeded in spades. We both know Curt is tough, both mentally and physically. Besides being brilliant, he grew up in a tough neighborhood where he probably settled more arguments with his sharp tongue than hard logic. Sure, he's been sarcastic and cynical with me. Even when you were in charge. But you know what...I think he managed himself more than I was ever aware of."

"Why do you say that?"

"I never saw his cynicism become a rallying cry for others. Even though he used it around me, he never pushed it in a way to enlist followers. He never seemed intent on spreading his negativity. He seemed to do it solely as a personal statement. In that respect, I think you did a great job. That's all I wanted to say. What was it you were about to say?"

Art, in his usual humility, said, "Oh, I just wanted to say you're right. I did fail with Curt. My hope was he would change. Become less sarcastic over time. I also let him get away with more than I should have. Sure, he never undermined anything important. For that I can consider myself moderately successful."

What Art said struck me as strange. I flashed back to all three meetings we'd had up till now. Where it all started was that first night at his house. Art began telling me his reasons for picking me for this job.

We talked about commitment. Then towards the end of the evening, he wrote down one of his key principles in practicing commitment: *Focus on what's important.* During the excursion on our bikes, he hit me with *Lead by example.* Then, at the Hollywood Bowl, we discussed *Reward success.*

What struck me as odd was all our previous discussions were different from the tone of what we were talking about today. This afternoon we concentrated on dealing with Curt. Our first three meetings all had such a very positive tone. Dealing with someone's sarcasm seemed so foreign. This was negative stuff. Was I wrong in thinking this way? I figured this would be a good question to ask, so I did.

"Not at all. You've hit the nail on the head," Art concurred. "Building and maintaining commitment is, for the most part, a positive activity with beneficial outcomes. Keeping focused, being an example, rewarding success—are all constructive. Real life, however, points out that all things are not positive. There are people who will undermine the commitment you believe is important…If you allow them to."

"Can some people undermine what you are trying to build without realizing what they're doing?"

"It happens all the time. Some people simply aren't aware of the impact of their behavior. Their negative comments and their sarcastic remarks are simply bad habits. Habits they are scarcely aware they have. Let's not forget there are others, though, who are fully aware of what they're doing. They show their disrespect consciously and deliberately."

"Curt, in my opinion, falls into the former category. He doesn't use his negativity consciously to undermine others."

"I definitely agree. He can be his own worst enemy. Curt's a good man. Everything he does, and I mean everything, is done with the right intent. His style is what gets in the way. Today's discussion is a good example of something we must watch for. Something that can dramatically influence commitment. What I'm trying to tell you is you also have to recognize and manage disrespect when it surfaces."

Somehow I knew this was a point worthy of inscription on my little scrap of paper at work. In my haste to meet Art this afternoon,

I forgot to grab it. I had meant to bring it along. Remembering now wasn't doing me much good.

"This is the keeper for today, isn't it?"

"The main one, yes." Studying my face, he added, "I've got a hunch you're thinking about that silly piece of paper you've become so attached to. The one on which you'd want me to record my latest pearl of wisdom. Well, you're out of luck today. I don't have any paper with me, either."

"Hey, come on. Are you trying to give me an opportunity to manage disrespect? I'll admit I'm overly attached to that piece of paper."

Art's smile told me I was a quick study.

So, I didn't expect an answer to my question. I continued, "Maybe I don't need the silly little piece of paper to remember what you've taught me. I've got it all up here," I grinned, tapping the side of my head.

"Etched in stone. My attachment to that piece of paper is purely sentimental. I've got my reasons for keeping it."

"Enough said," Art retorted. "It didn't take you long to apply today's lesson. Don't think I'm somehow above being sarcastic and cynical either. Even though I should know better, I fall into bad habits myself. Thanks for the reminder."

With so few opportunities to tease Art, I felt compelled to say, "So, even the almighty can be a cynic?"

"If not cynical, at least disrespectful. Our focus here has been Curt. His counterproductive behavior boils down to cynicism. Let's not forget there are a lot of other forms disrespect can take, forms more prevalent and harder to manage."

"Like what?" I responded.

"Like apathy. Like indifference. Like complacency. I wish this weren't true, but just look out there." He motioned toward the water. "What do you see?"

What I saw was beauty. The ocean was steel blue. White-caps dotted the bay as shadows from broken clouds cast subtle hues upon the water. You could distinguish Catalina Island rising majestically from the sea, a good forty miles from where we sat. There weren't many days when the island was so plainly visible from the mainland.

"I see a gorgeous view."

"Bingo!" Art shouted. "A million-dollar view if I've ever seen one. How often do you think we're afforded a view like this?"

"Oh, I'd say one day in thirty."

"If we're lucky. If you want an example of how big a problem disrespect can be, drive up and look at this view the other twenty-nine days. Mother Nature doesn't help the cause when she hides the pollution we dump on her. Santa Monica Bay is one of countless marine ecosystems that is straining under the load of human indifference and apathy. It's funny when we use the term *coastal development*. At this stage of the game, we should rename all building projects along the shore coastal destruction."

"It's eerie to think that on a day like today everything still looks so clean."

"Yet, the pollution is there. Under the surface. I'm about as upbeat a person as you'll find. About the only thing that scares me is the rate of disintegration our planet is experiencing. And, why is all this happening? Because man is disrespectful towards his own habitat."

What came to mind as Art depicted this seemingly wholesale disrespect was the phrase Harvard biologist E.O. Wilson coined: "the death of birth." He used the term to describe the pace at which we are driving entire ecosystems to extinction. Many of the rain forests, which historically served as the nurseries of new life forms, are disappearing quickly. Our apathy towards animal and plant life has produced frightening statistics. If my memory is correct, at the present rate—between plants and animals—we're averaging the loss of about one hundred species every day.

"I hate to think what you're saying is so fitting. You couldn't have picked a better example to make your point. I can see the kind of vocal cynicism we've been talking about with Curt is not the only kind of disrespect. As you said, it seems easier to deal with someone like Curt than the more subtle, more indifferent kind of person."

"When I think about all this, Sam, I feel inadequate. I haven't done enough personally. One of the underlying reasons I've left the corporate life is to devote more of my time to certain causes. Some of the things I hold dear suffer tremendously from people not managing disrespect. Take our youth. Look inside many of our high school classrooms and you see apathy in abundance. So many teenagers are simply turned off. I don't feel anyone in particular is to blame. At some level, I guess everyone has contributed…teachers, parents, administrators, the kids themselves. We haven't stepped up to the problem. When that happens, disrespect wins. What do you think happens to commitment when the forces of apathy gain momentum?"

"I guess all the good things done to build commitment can lose their effectiveness."

"You're a smart one, Sam. That's exactly what happens. What you see is snatching defeat right out of the jaws of victory. Everything done to effectively form and shape commitment can be lost. We've all experienced the point that it's far quicker and easier to knock down and destroy something than to build it up. What I'm trying to say is, if you really believe in something, you have to stand up to anyone whose actions jeopardize your commitment."

He was right. Strange to be talking about issues as big as the environment and have my mind wander to a small, personal one. Just last year we had our kitchen remodeled. I took responsibility for hiring the contractor. The workmen took exactly one day to tear the kitchen down. Then it took three months of eating out and microwave dinners before we had a functioning kitchen again. It amazed me how my contractor could lie so convincingly about how long the job would take. He sure took advantage of us. And, even with hindsight, he seemed better than the others who'd bid on the job.

Wait a minute! Remembering that fiasco with my contractor brings up an uncomfortable point. Everything Art had told me about commitment before today I consider myself good at. Sure, I've occasionally lost sight of what's important. Likewise, I've done a few things that weren't the best of examples. And, I've undoubtedly missed an opportunity or two to reward success.

Still, being less than perfect in these areas hadn't stopped me from believing I've lived up to Art's high expectations. On the other hand, today I feel we've uncovered a weakness…at least compared to everything else. For the first time since we began examining Art's meaning of commitment and why he picked me, I felt I didn't make the mark—truly inadequate…and guilty.

"I've got a confession to make on this one. My own recollection of standing up to people who show disrespect is not so great. I can think of lots of situations where I didn't stand up against someone showing disrespect. I should have, but I didn't. By doing nothing, I let them have a clear shot at subverting the situation."

"Don't be too hard on yourself, Sam. It's not easy to confront disrespect." Then, as if he thought better of it, he shot back, "On second thought, be hard on yourself. The easy route is to write off the cynics as incurable. Just see indifference as inevitable. Then you spend your life putting up with the aftermath of negativity. Managing disrespect is as important as anything we've talked about so far. Remember I'm carefully choosing my words here. What you are asked to do is manage disrespect. I didn't say your role is to cure or solve it."

"The word *manage* connotes an on-going process. Sam, in your job you're working with issues that have no permanent solutions. You work in an environment that is constantly changing. Respect—or for that matter, the lack of it—is never permanent. It can change by the minute. People who had respect yesterday can be turned off today. People full of disrespect today can become your biggest supporters tomorrow."

Art's comments got me to reflect, "Okay, I see the necessity of making sure disrespect, in whatever form it takes, is properly managed. There really is a cost in not confronting it. If you fail to eliminate disrespect over time, others can easily interpret this as you're not strongly committed. Or worse, it can signal you approve. In my own case, I've been an easy mark too many times. What got me thinking about my own inadequacy is the way I let a building contractor I hired to redo my kitchen practically bankrupt me. He'd whine, complain, feign apathy, show outright contempt...do anything but apologize for the delays and sloppy work."

A small smile began to form on Art's face. "Sounds like this guy knew every form of disrespect imaginable and how to get away with it. What was it in you that allowed him to get away with it?"

"Well, for one thing, I just don't like to deal with negative people. Generally, I wind up being more accommodating to them in a feeble attempt to avoid confrontations. I guess I find dealing with guys like that so distasteful I avoid it. I have a tendency to fall to their level when I do get fed up and I don't like this about myself, either...I know I have to improve in the way I deal with people who show disrespect. As a case in point, I'd like to talk more about how to handle Curt. Too many times in the past, I've taken too passive a stance when I saw someone taking potshots at what I'm committed to."

"Maybe you're right, Sam. This lesson is more important to you than the others. I believe you've truly learned the skills involved in keeping focused, leading by example, and rewarding success. You also have to skillfully step up to and manage anyone whose actions undermine that commitment. Let's use Curt as an example. If I weren't here to help, how would you get him to be more positive?"

"One thought is a rule I've used with my previous staff when we've found ourselves backed into a corner by a problem. When frustration began to bring out their negative sides, I'd institute the rule of 'No bitching about what isn't working—it's your responsibility to come up with positive alternatives instead.'"

"What do you mean when you say positive?" Art probed.

"By positive I mean come up with alternatives that are realistic, doable, and move us closer to a solution. The idea is to limit our options to only those that add value. I have found this has replaced complaining with more productive behavior."

"Okay. Apply this to Curt and the Special Olympics Program. What would your own rule suggest you do with Curt?"

"It's obvious. Challenge him to come up with a better way to recapture the spirit of involvement which he feels is no longer present." Seeing the sparkle in Art's eyes led me to say, "Why is everything so clear when I'm sitting on a hill overlooking the Pacific, but I'm a numbskull on the job?"

"Before you judge yourself brilliant up here on the bluff, finish the task. What else is appropriate to do with Curt or anyone else acting like he did?"

"Well, I guess for people like Curt, my *adding value* rule needs to apply all the time. Most people don't need that much correcting. For them such a rule can be used sparingly. Those like Curt need more constant reminding."

"I like your choice of words when you say *reminding*. What simple tool can you use to keep yourself and others focused on adding value?"

Applying the principles Art had reinforced was paying off. What immediately popped into my mind were the questions for keeping the right focus. With pride, I told him, "Through questions. By continually asking Curt questions about how his behavior benefits the customer, results, people, our values and management, I can steer the conversation in productive directions."

"You bet! Does this help the customer? Does this help achieve the results we want? Does this help our people perform more effectively? Does this help the organization? All these redirect the unaware cynic towards more productive behaviors. For conscious cynics, it forces the issue. They are exposed, which is how you want them. In the open is where they are easier to manage."

I felt better. I was seeing how my role went beyond demonstrating commitment myself to taking on the responsibility of instilling it in others.

"Thanks, Art. Coming up here I was really frustrated. Talking with you always seems to help clear my vision. Bottom line is, I know what I have to do tomorrow. More importantly, I see the need to develop my readiness to manage disrespect, whatever form it takes. Besides doing the things necessary to gain commitment, you also have to stand up to those doing the wrong things. Those choking off commitment."

"Like who?"

"I don't know what you mean, Art?"

"Like who else besides Curt? Or is he the only one needing your attention?"

"Right. I can't forget about Patty Simpson. She's about as vocal as Curt."

"Making sure people avoid doing the wrong things is equally as important as making sure people do the right things. *Focusing on what's important, Being an example, Rewarding success,* and *Managing disrespect*— together add up to a strong base of support toward your commitments. I know your positive nature, Sam. That's why it's easy for you to do the first three. Part of you doesn't want to hear that you also have to deal with negative issues like complacency or cynicism. Let me end today with a bit of good news. There are positive ways to manage disrespect. Mull that over during the holidays."

With that thought we ended our conversation on the bluff. The coast highway was one long line of cars. I was happy to be heading south toward home. In the oncoming traffic, I noticed the faces of the drivers. Some seemed angry. Others seemed bored and resigned. Fewer still seemed to enjoy the coastline view. Looking up, I saw the Eucalyptus perched near the edge of the bluffs. I wondered how well it was surviving the serpentine of cars winding along below.

At work the next day I was surprised to find a familiar note on my desk. It read: *Focus on What's Important, Lead by Example, Reward Success,* and *Manage Disrespect.* I had to wonder how he got it there so quickly.

You can do very little with faith, but you can do nothing without it.

— Samuel Butler

Chapter 6

FOCUS ON THE UNIMPORTANT

Business slows down during the two weeks before the New Year. The result is a more relaxed atmosphere than during the normal workload. Taking advantage of the lull, I spent most of my time walking around and talking with employees. The contact I was able to have during the holiday period was invaluable, well worth not taking any vacation time myself.

Now that January was here, I was ready for a rest. Over the six months I'd been in the top spot, I scarcely remember taking a full day off, even on weekends. I decided to indulge myself with a ski trip. What better way to get away than a trip to the mountains? I don't know if it's the air, the scenery, the physical challenge, or the whole package that makes ski trips so enjoyable to me. I packed up the family and headed for a week at a favorite spot of ours in western Canada.

Sitting by the fire on the fifth day of my trip, I was quietly interrupted by the proprietress of the inn. She asked if I wanted to take a phone call from a gentleman named Art Brunsing. Over the many years I have come to the Ram's Head Inn, it has taken on the feeling of a second home. The Butlers who run the place never forget the purpose of our visits. While on vacation, they believe guests should be on vacation. They have served as a welcome buffer for me against outside pressures like phone calls from work. This was one of the things I've enjoyed most about the place. It's pure. No mixing of business and pleasure. A stay at the Ram's Head Inn is all relaxation and recreation.

Normally I wouldn't take any calls that weren't family matters. Art, needless to say, falls into a unique category. He is one of the few people I'd let interrupt my stay. So, I got up and went into the kitchen to take the call.* One feature of the Inn is there are no phones in the guest rooms. This coincides with the ambience of the place. You come here to ski some of the best terrain in North America, not to spend time chatting on the phone.

I had to admit it was nice hearing Art's cheery voice, "Guess we've both got the same idea. I tried reaching you at home and at work. By twisting an arm or two I was told of your whereabouts in Rossland."

Instantly I knew whose arm he'd twisted. Marcie, my assistant and formerly Art's, was the only one who knew my exact whereabouts. Even though she knew I'd have given her permission to divulge my whereabouts to Art, I figured I'd give her a good-natured ribbing when I returned to L.A. Chuckling to myself, I almost missed what Art said next.

"I called to see if you wanted to join me for some skiing here in Tahoe. How much longer are you going to be up there?"

"Not long enough. Only two more days. Then it's back to reality. What makes it so tough is the snow's been fabulous. The storm pattern is dropping a foot of powder every third day or so. Just when the mountain is getting skied out, a fresh storm comes in and blankets the area. Tomorrow afternoon we should get another good dump. At least my last day will be perfect."

Art surprised me with his rather matter of fact, "Mind if I join you? That is, if I'm not interrupting any family plans."

---

* In 1989 when this book was written, cell phones were in their infancy. Today we have to deal with 7/24 accessibility/interruptions.

He explained a day skiing together would be a great setting for the new direction our meetings would be taking. When I asked where he was skiing, he told me he was staying at the Ski-Inn Lodge. I asked him if it would be more convenient for me to meet him in California on my way south. Under different conditions, he would have agreed. His willingness to make such a big sacrifice boiled down to my glowing forecast of the local snow conditions at Red Mountain.

We decided he would fly up tomorrow and we'd ski together the next day. This would be fun. The only other time I'd skied with Art was during an executive retreat he put on a few years ago. We'd ski until early afternoon. After that, we'd hold our meetings. Dinner would be pushed back a little later than normal in order to put in a good day's work. I remember those meetings being exceptionally productive. Wonder why we did it only once? Maybe I'd ask him about it when he got up here.

Walking out of the kitchen, I returned to my cozy seat near the fire. The sixteen or so guests at the inn generally idle away the time between a full day's skiing and dinner by reading or chatting with one another. This usually takes place here in the common room, dominated by a huge stone fireplace. The meals are served at tables lining two walls of this same room. Above the tables, the windows look out on a thick wooded glen. Discernable through this canopy are Red and Granite Mountains rising sharply as a noticeable backdrop to the lovely panorama.

Glancing at the roaring fire, I thought back to the end of my last meeting with Art. He had given me something to mull over during the holidays. The seed he had planted in my mind was a positive way to manage disrespect. I remember leaving our meeting place overlooking the Pacific bent on finding out how to accomplish this. If there was an answer, a positive way to influence people who had become complacent or cynical, I was determined to find it. My plan was to try out whatever I came up with on Curt before Art and I met again.

Art's question had stuck in my mind like a dripping faucet. After coercing myself to incubate on the matter for a couple of days, I wound up with an interesting idea on how to deal with Curt's sarcasm. The results of my somewhat novel approach had been promising so far. I'm sure Art would feel the same. Funny how I had safely locked it out of my conscious mind during my ski week. Now I found myself anxious to see Art and discuss what I've done to manage disrespect.

Knowing I'd be skiing with Art on my last day, I had to change my immediate plans. Normally I'd ski the last day with any member of the family who wanted to come along with Randy and Phil. Randy owns the ski school and Phil is his top instructor. I think they enjoy skiing with me for comic relief.

No matter how good a skier I've become over the years, they'd find places to take me where I'd wind up slightly over my head. In other words, I'd find myself in trouble. My goal in skiing has always been to be like them. They seem to be able to ski any terrain, any condition, in control. Some day I'm going to be able to say that about my own skiing.

Given their laid back demeanor, it wasn't too hard for them to switch their schedules. By late afternoon, the snow was beginning to float down between the trees. After boasting to Art about the clockwork precision of the snowfall, I was especially glad to see it coming down. After a few runs, we decided to do a little ski touring and I was taken to a new part of the mountain. My adventuresome kids had skied up here before. We wound up descending a slope where my skills were, shall I say, slightly lacking. Phil always told me if I wasn't falling, I wasn't putting any learning into the gray matter. One point he continually stressed was the need to stretch your limits if you're going to advance. If Phil was right, once again my brain was overflowing.

Whenever I went out with these guys, I'd wind up drained. Between laughing, falling, and skiing as hard as I could to keep up with everyone, I barely had the energy to walk the two hundred yards back to the inn. Trudging over the little rise immediately behind the inn, I spotted the red metal roof nestled in the trees. Since dusk was rapidly approaching, I wondered if Art had arrived.

I looked up to see what was being served for dinner as I passed through the front doors. Dave prints the menu on a small chalkboard by the kitchen door. Once you've stayed at the inn, you develop a conditioned response. There is no way to walk by the chalkboard without stopping to read what's for dinner. Tonight it read:

Grilled Leg of Lamb
Scalloped Potatoes Minted Peas
Ginger Carrots & Snitz Pear
& Gooseberry Pie

Great, one of my favorites. Doreen's meals are so good the guests spend an inordinate amount of time talking about her cooking. As I passed by the Dutch door of the kitchen, Doreen called out that my friend had arrived. I thanked her for the information and her dinner selection. Passing into the main room of the inn, I spotted Art on the sofa, beer in hand, reading a ski magazine. Sneaking up behind him, I gave him a playful punch on the shoulder and exclaimed, "You old buzzard, how you doing?"

Without lifting an eye from the page, he replied, "Couldn't be better. Doreen told me you were out on the mountain scouting some new runs. Hope you don't run me ragged out there tomorrow." Then looking up he added, "Can I buy you a beer? They're right out the door in the snow."

The only thing not provided at the inn is liquor. Guests take care of their own needs in this department. This is the only thing I can think of not provided to guests. Beer and wine are usually stashed right outside the back door in the snow. Art had bought a twelve pack of Kooteney, a local brew, and had neatly stored it in the snow bank within easy reach of the door. Checking to see if he needed a refill, I grabbed two bottles and sat down in front of the fire.

"Hey, great seeing you up here, Art. My favorite ex-boss at my favorite ski mountain. Kris and the kids will be happy to see you. Here's to a super day of skiing tomorrow."

As I tipped my beer toward Art's, he clicked his bottle against mine. We drank a toast to the soft, dry powder snow drifting softly down outside. The iced beer cooled my parched throat. "So you've met Doreen and Dave, have you?"

"Sam, I feel like they've known me from birth. You must have told them everything good there is to know about me a dozen times over. Didn't seem to impress 'em much, though…Doreen still made me wipe off my shoes before letting me in.

Dave gave me an escorted tour around the inn while explaining the rules. They're the kind of people who aren't awed by anyone's reputation. Seems like the only impressive thing I've done is know you. I see why you like the place so much."

"As you know, it's really the people who make a place special. Besides great skiing, what makes me travel all the way up here is the uncomplicated, good-natured sense of the people. They're really nice folk."

As I was speaking, Dave announced dinner. Concluding, I said, "No, on second thought, the reason I like this place so much is the food. Wait and see for yourself."

Dinner was a feast. While we ate, there was no indication Art was thinking about our last conversation. Talk centered on skiing. Dinner seemed reminiscent of our first dinner at Art's house. I had wanted to talk business but Art wouldn't let me until later in the study. I was controlling my impatience better this time.

After we finished, Art and I moved to the sofa. The kids went downstairs to play Ping-Pong. Kris sat down to a game of hearts with some of the other guests. Art and I interspersed talking with other guests and tidbits of private conversation. Sitting in front of the crackling fire with a full stomach felt almost decadent.

I never tire of finding myself in front of a good fire. Even with stimulating conversation, I am easily mesmerized watching the flames work on themselves, slowly consuming the energy in the logs. Watching the glowing embers drop to the hearth bed, I found it easy to bide my time. Despite my tendency to jump right in, I wanted Art to be the one to turn the conversation to commitment.

Fortunately, he didn't take long. Almost as an aside, he inquired if I had talked to Curt. This was exactly what I hoped he'd ask. In my estimation, the change in Curt was almost miraculous. He had come a long way fast. Sure it was too early to conclude he wouldn't revert to his old ways. But, I wanted to tell Art all about it. My enthusiasm to talk bothered me, though. I've never really felt Art's equal. Succeeding where he had not certainly fed my ego. I wanted to be careful not to boast.

"Curt seems to have reacted well when I confronted him. First, I told him I was aware of your previous discussions with him on sarcasm. I said I wasn't happy with his failure to change his behavior. What I did next sprang from our conversation sitting above the Getty Museum.

I asked him for his own suggestions on how someone could help him reduce the frequency of these remarks. I figured I might as well make him choose his own cure.

What Curt came up with surprised me. He suggested a technique that worked for him when he quit smoking. Based on what he described, we went out and bought a big glass jar. Curt then put it on his desk. The jar was to serve as a container for five-dollar bills, and Curt would stuff in a five for each sarcastic remark he made. We devised a list of key people who would try to catch him making negative remarks. Curt even volunteered his own name for the list. He was willing to catch himself being cynical, too. Can you believe that?"

Art was amused by my tale. His riveted attention to the details of my narrative matched his smile, which was glowing brighter than the fire. He begged for information on how things were working so far. I was happy to oblige.

"The first week the jar put a major dent in Curt's wallet. This gave us some pretty conclusive evidence he really hadn't been controlling this behavior. Then, the contributions began to taper off. It looked like he was beginning to become more conscious of what he said. Half way through the second week, I decided to get more involved. I felt we could make a game of it.

In my mind poor Curt was doing all the work. I wasn't really adding much value. Anyway, I thought why not have some fun with this thing. Together we counted the money. Then I challenged Curt to a contest. If over the next month he could keep from doubling the current amount in the pot, I would personally contribute $500 to his favorite charity.

He took the bet with a sarcastic smile on his face. So I made him put five bucks in the jar. Right on the spot, I made him do it. Having stuck my neck out, I didn't want him to think this would be easy."

Art commented that he was sure my motives were purely altruistic. We both laughed at that.

"From what I could forecast before leaving for skiing, I'd be out the $500 unless Curt had a major setback. I was glad I wasn't there to protect my investment by baiting him."

Art was thrilled with my report. He said he could kick himself for not coming up with a similar plan for Curt. He then asked where the money in the jar was going. I told him it would go to my favorite charity: The Art Brunsing Scholarship Fund. Art seemed a bit embarrassed. Then, as if to try and hide his feelings he took the offensive by saying, "That's great. Now I'm sure you've heard what's good for the goose is good for the gander. How about applying this system you've concocted on ourselves?"

We ended the evening by agreeing to try Curt's program starting first thing in the morning. Knowing ourselves pretty well, we realized skiing together would bring out our competitive juices. And, competition in the past had often been accompanied by jocular sarcasm.

Before going to bed, I put several five-dollar bills in my parka, just in case. Sleep came easy. The cumulative effect of five days of hard skiing with my family was beginning to show on my body. Before I knew it, morning came. Brilliant sunshine reflecting off snow-covered peaks greeted the early riser. The view was even more inviting than the smell of the inn's morning coffee.

A sense of restrained excitement filled the breakfast tables. To say Art's and my exhilaration exceeded the inn's other fanatical skiers would be misleading. We all hurried through the meal, feigning a cavalier atti-tude toward the virgin snow beckoning outside. Underneath we were all plotting to be the first one up the mountain to get untracked powder.

Neither Art nor I slowed the other when getting our gear. I already had our lift tickets. We headed directly to the Granite chair twenty min-utes before it was scheduled to start operation. From the inn, only my kids beat us to the lift. We still wound up behind two dozen hardcore Rosslanders, though. Thankfully, even with a hundred more skiers, we'd still be able to carve virgin powder for a good part of the morning.

All the way up the lift, I pointed out the various options we had for skiing down the front of the mountain. When we hit the top, we headed for one of the out-of-bounds areas that promised maiden tracks. The skiing couldn't have been better. If enjoyment were the only pre-requisite, Art and I would qualify for the Olympics. Our first couple of uninterrupted runs was indescribable.

On our fourth trip up the mountain, our adrenalin surge began to weaken. Our frenzy to imprint new tracks on the snow started to evaporate. Art was the one to turn the conversation to our favorite topic. He started off by saying we were at a crossroads in our meetings. I wasn't sure what he meant.

Before allowing me a chance to ask, he requested I summarize all I had learned about commitment from our prior talks. The four sup-porting behaviors were easy to remember. I had them memorized. The paper I kept on my desk had served its purpose well.

In reviewing the essence of what I had learned, I started with defin-ing commitment. I told him commitment required both believing in something and acting consistent with that belief. The definition I liked best was Art's description of commitment as "persistence with a purpose." Then, I went on to summarize the key actions that show someone is supporting their commitments: focusing on what's important, leading by example, rewarding success, and managing disrespect.

Art reinforced my last point, "Yes, it's critical to manage those who have developed what we could call negative commitment. Namely, a cynical mistrust of customers, how the organization operates, coworkers, other departments, or how results are accomplished. This is the opposite of having a positive commitment. People who have negative commitment use the same four behaviors we've talked about. Unfortunately, they use them in a destructive way."

His words reminded me of his challenge from our last meeting to find a positive way to manage disrespect. This time I didn't want this thought to slip away by letting the conversation take a different turn. The way I had handled Curt seemed very positive to me. I wonder how close my handling of this situation was to what had been on Art's mind.

Art had started skiing down Southern Belle, one of the runs taking us to an area of the mountain called Paradise. Chasing him, we skied about a third of the way down before he stopped. As I pulled alongside, he said, "I'm pleased with what you've absorbed from our conversations. One of the more difficult lessons is the realization true support means standing up for what you believe in. I've been thinking about what you said last night...what you've done with Curt."

Finally, I had my chance to ask what he meant by a positive approach to managing disrespect. "Was what I did with Curt on target?"

He responded instantly, "Yes it was. Last night anyone listening to our conversation would have said so. Without knowing much about what we were talking about, they would have known. How? They could tell by your voice."

"What do you mean?"

"I want you to think back before our meeting last month. Go even further back to the meeting with your staff where you discussed the company's involvement with Special Olympics. You weren't exactly happy then, were you? I'm sure Curt had been cynical even before then. Right? Compare how you feel now with how you felt then. Before we met, what had you done about the situation?"

Art knew the answer. All I did about Curt's cynicism was let it fester. I remember being reluctant to challenge him.

"By doing nothing, Sam, you were giving tacit approval for his actions. To anyone observant enough to notice, you would have come across as apathetic or, at best, unaware of what was happening. I'm sure you don't feel great about your actions now. Am I right?"

"Sure, Art. I admit I wasn't adding much value by letting his skepticism and disbelief ruin things."

"Certainly not a positive way to manage the situation. On the other hand, what did you do after our little afternoon meeting?"

"I told myself to find a positive way to turn Curt around. I wanted to find a way, any way, to help him be committed in a positive manner."

"What I'd like to know is how you came up with the splendid solution you implemented?"

After thinking for a bit, I responded, "I really can't put my finger on what I did, except…I kept thinking about it. At odd times I would find myself trying to find an answer I hadn't thought of before. Most of the time, I'd quit without making any progress. To my credit, I suppose, I persisted.

One day it simply popped into my head. Why not ask Curt how to change his own behavior. For all his faults, dishonesty was not one of them. Maybe he'd make my job easier by pointing out what I was overlooking. Since I was having such a hard time formulating a solution myself, I felt I had nothing to lose."

"If I hear you right, what you consciously decided to do was look for a better way. You were trying to improve the situation, not resigning yourself and giving up. What you did was exactly what I mean by a positive approach to managing disrespect. If you are really committed to something, you go beyond supporting it. You take the next step and try to improve on it.

If you are determined to improve a situation, like you were here, you shift gears mentally. This act, by itself, is the positive approach I was alluding to at the end of our last meeting. Striving to improve on the current situation is inherently positive. And, unless I'm wrong, you felt good about trying. Even before you came up with something. Am I right?"

He was right. He pushed me to describe what it was I actually did. It may seem obvious, but the first thing I did was to make a conscious decision to find a better way. That step occurred before I left the bluff at the Getty Museum. Before I made this commitment, all I had been doing was commiserating with myself. My only action was to tell myself something was wrong. Art motivated me to take positive action. From that point, I was actively seeking a better approach.

"As far as I can see, the first step on the road to improvement is consciously choosing to look for a better way. If you don't look yourself, you're at the mercy of random chance. A valuable improvement may lie in the path ahead, yet you fail to see it. If you do stumble across it, you can only thank luck."

Art agreed wholeheartedly. Most of us want to see positive change. Yet, how many set aside time to take the steps necessary for improvement to actually occur?

"You know, Art, I didn't notice it at the time. As you pointed out, when I was struggling to find a positive way with Curt, I honestly felt better. Even when I was frustrated. Before trying to improve the situation, I was really no different than he was. His disrespect may have been actively played out, but mine was more passive and harder to detect. I was complacent. I lacked the spirit to be committed. Then, just by trying to find an answer, I felt commitment again. I had a purpose. And, I gained the energy to *persist with a purpose.*"

Art listened conscientiously until he knew I was finished. Then, as he began to ski away, he said, "What you replaced your complacency with was curiosity. A much more productive state of mind."

Skiing down the first groomed run of the day, we cruised the rest of the way down to the Paradise chair lift.

"Lack of curiosity kills commitment."

"One of my favorite lines is attributed to Professor Porsche as he was conducting a tour of all the fabulous automobiles his company had built over the years. Someone asked. 'Which of these outstanding cars is your favorite?' His answer was beautiful: *'I haven't built it yet.'*"

We poled our way to the loading point as our turn arrived for the trip up the mountain. Settling in for the ride, Art continued, "You see, Sam, commitment is a blend of supporting what exists and striving to improve upon it. Neither alone is enough. Showing commitment only through supporting behaviors is a little naive. The danger in only supporting is a tendency over time for stagnation. Remember, though, showing support is vital in demonstrating genuine commitment. And, instilling it in others. What is needed in addition is the excitement of seeking a better future.

"That brings us to another kind of person. What do you think happens with the person who is out of balance because he or she only pushes for improvements? Never supports anything?"

"They are the ones who project that good is never good enough. They always expect more. By refusing to support anything, I'd think the tone would become negative eventually. People burn out under constant pressure. By never stopping to count the victories and celebrate the successes, motivation soon dries up."

Heading up the mountain, I started to feel a few pieces coming together. Art had drilled the supporting behaviors into me. Now we were off on a new adventure, a new direction. Art was taking me on a new mental adventure, just like Randy and Phil often took me to new terrain to ski. The understanding between us led to a period of silence.

Art intruded on the silence by saying, "As you've probably guessed, our next couple of meetings will focus on how to instill commitment through a whole new set of behaviors. As I hoped you would, you took my bait and used Curt as a vehicle to practice the next concept. You succeeded with Curt because you chose to be dissatisfied with the present situation. You also chose to change things in a constructive fashion. As you already said, the first step in improving anything is looking for a better way. This is what I wanted to reinforce on this trip."

I could tell by his voice that this was the focal point of today's discussion. Looking for a better way. I began to wonder where else I should be looking for a better way.

"So, where should I look for a better way, besides Curt? Where is my time best spent trying to improve things?"

Art responded with two propositions. "Well, you could look at what's not working. Such as you did with Curt. Or, you could look at something you're perfectly happy with."

Nothing like stringing together two opposites. I know my instincts would be seduced into focusing on current problems, especially the more pressing ones. Most likely I'd spend my time looking there. Problems, where we readily experience dissatisfaction, have a way of hogging a great deal of our creative attention. Posing the possibility of looking at what I'm happy with was an interesting idea. It opened a host of new possibilities.

After quickly sorting through a number of them, I carefully postulated, "Maybe given what you said about looking at what you're perfectly happy with, I'd spend my time looking for a better way with what is most important to me."

When he didn't immediately respond, I felt a need to explain, "I haven't forgotten the key point you made that first night in your study: *focus on what's important*. We both know for the CEO this means supporting our values. Couldn't it be productive for me to look for better ways to implement our corporate values?"

His eyes brightened. Yet, he was still in deep thought. He was contemplating what I had said very deliberately. "I apologize for not saying anything sooner. A good answer requires diligent reflection. Your answer was so good it's uncanny. Unfortunately for me, I wasn't prepared for it. I'd already thought through what I was going to say next. Now it seems somewhat inappropriate. You blew my train of thought."

Glancing up, I noticed we were passing the last tower. The unloading point at the top was rapidly approaching. I shouted in a panic, "That's not the only thing we'll blow! Get your tips up!"

My warning barely allowed us enough time to negotiate the ramp without a mishap. Skiing off to the side to adjust our equipment I felt a little self-conscious. After all these years of skiing, falling off the lift was not something I expected or looked forward to doing. Art's face telegraphed the same sheepishness.

I was about to insult him when I remembered our pact about five dollar remarks. Out of the side of my mouth I piped, "We better not forget what we came here to do." Extending my hand out and holding my thumb and forefinger about an inch apart, I continued, "Nothing like coming this close to an embarrassing mishap."

Art's pleasure at my remark seemed greater than the quip deserved. "What's so funny?" I asked.

"Oh, poetic justice I guess. Not only did you blow the brilliant line of reasoning I was about to deliver, you caught me so off guard I forgot we were on a chair lift."

"Sorry. I didn't mean to wreak havoc on your concentration. Maybe we should backtrack a bit. What astute observation did I blow for you?"

"When I turned your question about where to look for a better way back on you, your answer was to focus on what's most important. This dumbfounded me. Then, you continued to drive nails into the coffin of my prepared retort by explaining you'd focus on a better way to implement our values."

"This wasn't what you'd hoped I'd say?"

"Not at all. It was the greatest of answers. I was too caught up in formulating a play on words. I was trying to be really clever. I was going to suggest when you're looking for a better way, it's often best to focus on what's unimportant—not so clever a remark based upon your answer. What a twisted mess, huh?"

He wasn't kidding. I was genuinely confused. Focusing on what's important has become one of my most cherished beliefs. Art's too, unless everything up till now was an elaborate set up. I doubted that. Why would he now come up with such a seemingly contrary principle? Snapping the last buckle on my boot, I stood up and started to stretch some stiff muscles as I waited for Art.

What ingenious trick was he up to? What he said couldn't conflict more with my answer of looking at our values. How could he agree so whole-heartedly with my answer and have been getting ready to say *focus on what's unimportant*? I could see why he had been dumbstruck on the chair lift.

"What were you driving at with a comment like focus on the unimportant?"

As he finished stretching, Art began to explain. "Let me try and reconstruct my logic for you, Sam. When you first asked about where to look for a better way, do you remember what I said?"

I remembered he hadn't answered me. Instead he had given me two choices. "You answered me with a couple of options: Look for making improvements where I was dissatisfied. Or, look where I was perfectly happy."

"How are those two options different, Sam?"

"The obvious answer is they're different in the degree of satisfaction one has regarding what you are looking at…"

"Anything else? Anything not so obvious?"

What immediately struck me was the word obvious. When looking for a better way, it seems obvious to look where you're dissatisfied. It's less obvious to look at what you're happy with. In fact, it is those things you might easily take for granted.

"I think these two options differ in how obvious they are to the task; the task being looking for a better way."

Art gave his characteristic nod—the kind of nod that showed he especially approved of what was just said.

"Now you're reaching a key distinction. One worthy of more exploration. Which of these two options normally appears to be more important?"

I was beginning to understand what he was driving at by *focusing on what's unimportant*. Where does our mind put things we are content with, that are working flawlessly? On the back burner. Out of sight, out of mind.

"You sly devil. Human nature would suggest we tend to focus on what's not working, what's causing us pain, suffering, and grief. These problems, if you want to call them that, crowd our thinking and become critically important by default. What we are happy with is a lower priority. Out of sight, out of mind.

What we are not thinking about has a hard time achieving an important status. So, let me guess what you're driving at. When you said *focus on the unimportant*, you really meant to look for better ways with those things we are already happy with. Am I right?"

"As right as the fact we're standing on a mountain top. The clever twist I was trying to make so eloquently lies in a deeper understanding of what I was referring to with the word *unimportant*. We all get trapped by mental barriers to creative thinking. What we perceive as important at any given point may not be what's important at all. You know your answer really did reinforce the point I was trying to make. Your timing is what stunk."

Aha! Art was the first to blow it. A five-dollar fine was in the making. "Oh, excuse me, Art. Did you say *stunk*? Isn't that a bit sarcastic? I think you owe me a fiver. Got it on you?"

"No!" was all he could muster.

"That's okay. I know you're good for it. You can pay me later. Maybe we better get back to what we came here for. We didn't come just to talk."

Art agreed. I led him to one of my favorite routes down the mountain. The path descends through thick tree cover to a series of wide-open powder fields. At a choice spot offering a panorama view of the neighboring peaks, we took a breather.

I took this opportunity to tell Art he could only blame himself for my answer. My own common sense, or lack thereof, would have looked for a better way where results weren't achieving our expectations. It was his clue about considering what I was happy with that led me to focus on the corporate values. We both concurred that common sense recognizes it may be much more useful and profitable to improve what you are happy with. There is where the truly important issues often lie.

Being tired, we agreed this would be the last run down the mountain. We didn't say much as we trudged with our gear back to the Ram's Head. Sitting with feet propped by the fire, Art summed up the day, "Today was the best yet. I really enjoyed myself. I would have travelled twice as far for the skiing we did today. There couldn't be a better place to discuss the importance of looking for a better way. Since this was your idea, why don't you pick the time and place for our next meeting?"

Funny, I didn't remember this being my idea. Coming up here was supposed to be my vacation. Not that I'd change a thing, mind you. Today was great. The skiing was superb.

And, the conversation's new direction intrigued me. How does Art do it? I'm the one who called our last meeting to talk about Curt. Yet everything we discussed seems to follow some predetermined pattern with Art at the controls. Then again, maybe I'm reading too much into things. Art's real knack is his ability to use whatever's happening around him to make his point.

I shifted my focus to his suggestion. Where would be a good place to meet next time? Next month is February. I love winter sunsets in Santa Monica Bay. And, winter is the only time of year the sun sets directly over the water there. This creates magnificent postcard sunsets you don't see in summer months.

"Why don't we keep ourselves flexible on the date. Let's have a picnic on the beach when the conditions are right?"

A long, drawn out "perfect" was his reply. While I was gazing at the fire—thinking about our next rendezvous spot, a thought from a couple of nights ago presented itself.

"Art, why did you take your staff to the Ski-Inn Lodge only once? The experience was not a lot different from today. I remember it being both exceptionally fun and profitable, too."

What Art said next kind of surprised me. "We only went once because it was so successful. I would have done it again if we hadn't achieved so much. Any future meeting there would have been judged by what we accomplished before in terms of enjoyment and results. My guess was any future meeting wouldn't measure up.

This forced me into a situation of having to look for a better way sooner than I would have if the first meeting was less successful. To achieve the same outcomes we did at the Ski-Inn Lodge required a new setting. You see whether we want it or not, success does not insulate us from the need to improve things. It can actually accelerate the pace."

*The trouble with experience as a teacher is that the
test comes first and the lesson afterwards.*

— McFadden's Observation

Chapter 7
FOLLOW THE LEAD

Curiosity is a sure antidote for complacency. When you're actively looking for something, it's amazing what happens to your perception. Your awareness substantially improves. For instance, when you're not looking for a perfect sunset and one catches you by surprise, you can fool yourself into thinking such occurrences happen more frequently than they actually do. I wouldn't have believed how many days went by waiting for conditions that promised a colorful sunset.

Heading in an easterly direction, last night's storm added about half-an-inch toward reducing our drought conditions. The remnants of the storm promised to stay with us long enough to affect tonight's sunset. Finally, the time seemed right. With a sky adorned by a broken bank of cumulus clouds and a sea cast a deep blue by the recent turbulence, I called Art to see about our planned rendezvous. His exact words were "ready, willing and able."

In exchange for my supplying the food, he agreed to bring a blanket to sit on and some beach chairs. Our agreed-upon meeting place was the second jetty north of Santa Monica Canyon. Hanging up the phone, I packed my briefcase and headed for the Palisades. Weeks earlier, I had packed some sweats in the trunk of my car to change into once I reached the parking lot. A business suit feels out of character for the beach, even when no one was around to see you.

My plan was to stop along the way at the Gourmet Gala and have them pack us a dinner basket. I've shopped there enough to trust their quality. I don't even bother picking things out anymore. Everything's so tasty. Angela and Rosemary, the women who fix the baskets, are far more creative than I am when it comes to the culinary arts. Walking in the door, I spotted Rosemary behind the counter. "How's business, Rosemary?"

"Busy as usual. You should have seen the place a couple of hours ago. You'd think we were giving away winning lottery tickets. How've you been, anyway? Haven't seen you for awhile."

"Been busy myself. Just dropped by for you to fix a dinner basket. Pick out what fancies you. It's for two."

"Oh, you and Kris having a romantic evening without the kids? Want something special?"

By the tone of her voice, I could tell she was drawing the wrong conclusion. Better correct her mistake or she might outdo herself and try to add a spice of romance in the packaging.

"Not that kind of special. This is a close business associate. One who does deserve first-class treatment."

"Okay. Can I fix you a cappuccino while you wait?"

Sounded too good to pass up. As she fixed the basket, we engaged in small talk about the neighborhood. Angela came out of the back room where she was working and joined the conversation. Once the basket was prepared, I gulped down the rest of my cappuccino and bid them goodbye.

Storing the provisions in the trunk and transferring my sweats to the seat next to me, I headed straight for the beach. We were supposed to meet at four thirty. Glancing at my watch, I figured I'd make it to the parking lot a couple of minutes early. I always liked being on time.

Art's car wasn't there yet. In fact there wasn't a single car parked along the section of beach where three jetties, spaced about three hundred yards apart, carved a bit more character into the coastline. Upon arrival, my first priority was changing clothes. With no one around, the car made a good place to change. Scarcely had I pulled on my sweatpants when I heard Art's car pull up behind me. I had been wrestling with whether to wear my Rockports or go barefoot. With Art's arrival I decided it must be an omen to leave the shoes off.

Grabbing our gear, we trudged over the sand to a spot near the water. The sand still radiated faint warmth from the afternoon sun. It crunched a little underfoot. Maybe the top half-inch or so had dried from the afternoon sun. Underneath, the sand still held a good deal of moisture from last night's rainfall. One didn't have to be Sherlock Holmes to detect we were the first to walk this expanse of beach since the storm. I always liked making the first footprints on a fresh stretch of sand erased of any sign of prior encroachment.

A light breeze was coming on shore. The salty air really hits you when you haven't been close to the sea for a while. The sound of waves breaking near shore and the smell of salt always bring back happy memories. Every time I'm here, I feel young again. Most of my youth was spent hanging out as a local along this stretch of coastline.

"Smells good...doesn't it?"

Art agreed. Experience allowed the two of us to deftly spread the blanket, working with the breeze instead of against it. After positioning the basket, chairs, and the other articles we brought along for warmth, we sat down facing the water. Looking at Art, I inquired whether he had spent much time at the beach.

"Yes. I used to come a lot when my kids were growing up. Over the summer they would pester me to go to the beach. After I got used to coming down, I found I loved it. At first I thought there'd be nothing to do. Once I started coming fairly regularly, I found a lot to do."

"Funny, my experience was different. More like your kids. As a kid, I practically lived here. As an adult, I moved away from the beach life."

"Grew up a local, huh?"

"You bet. Right down there." I pointed to the stretch of beach about a half-mile to the south. Just as I was putting my arm down Art noticed something out in the water.

Excited, he exclaimed, "Look! Fins! Do you think they're sharks?" Sure enough, there was a large school of dolphins swimming toward us from the south. Their path mirrored the coastline about thirty yards from shore.

"Good eyes, Art! I hadn't seen 'em. They're not sharks. They're Pacific dolphins. When they surface again, look at the front of the head. There, see. Notice the cup-like protrusion where the mouth is."

He was like a kid. He'd jumped to his feet and was staring at the mammals as they lazily skimmed the surface, moving up the coast. I told him this was a good time of year to see them. With the summer beach crowd gone, they fished a lot closer to shore.

His interest kept him on his feet until the dolphins swam a couple of hundred yards north of us. He asked me what I knew about them and if I'd ever been in the water with them. I had to admit his enthusiasm was contagious. Dolphins are such noble creatures. Art's fervor brought up an old fantasy I have about encountering dolphins in the wild.

To be close enough in their own natural habitat to communicate by touch and gesture was my unfulfilled dream. Unfortunately, when I've been in the water near dolphins, they've kept a safe distance. As we nestled back on the blanket, I noticed the sun beginning the last leg of its journey to the horizon.

"Sitting between land and sea, the sun setting in the distance, always brings out the philosopher in me. How about you, Art?"

"It has that tendency. Mother Nature is a master mood-setter. She has an immense capacity to touch an inner chord. People come to land's end for everything from inspiration to consolation. Mother Nature sets a great stage to use for our own purposes."

"Yes, and she really knows how to put on a show."

The golden edges of the sun were beginning to radiate oranges and pinks, illuminating thin strands of stratus that would otherwise be invisible. Watching the ever-changing show, I began to reflect out loud on our conversation from last month.

"Last time we talked about improving things and looking for a better way. Often in my life when really searching for something, I've wound up here on the beach. I especially love this time of year when you have the place to yourself. The summer crowds are gone. It really makes you feel part of something bigger, something grander. Walking alone along the shoreline, has led to some of my most creative insights."

"This may be true. But, it reminds me of something I once read: 'If you know the enemy and know yourself, you need not fear the result of a hundred battles. If you know yourself, but not the enemy, for every victory gained you will also suffer one defeat. If you know neither the enemy nor yourself, you will succumb in every battle.'"

"Isn't that from *The Art of War?*"

"Yes…the words of Sun Tzu."

"Why on earth did you bring that up?"

"To remind you of something. Certainly we can gain wonderful insight in solitude. Yet, the best we can do here is know ourselves better. On the other hand, it is what we learn from others that lead to our greatest victories. Certainly all experience offers some lesson. Even a solitary stroll on the beach. Yet, when you think about your most valuable lessons, how often does it come from solitude? And, how often has it come from experiences involving others?"

Contemplating what he said, I had to admit most of what I've learned of real importance was from others. I guess I had been lucky to have a number of people who taught me a lot. Even as a kid on the beach, for all the dropouts and deviates, there were a handful of older guys who gave me a new perspective on what was important in life. These older locals were not people who made it rich in any monetary sense. Some of them were schoolteachers. They loved the extra leisure their profession gave them to spend more than a normal amount of time on the beach.

"I have to agree with you and Sun Tzu. A much wiser approach is to learn from others as well as yourself. Even your enemies are a storehouse of valuable insight…As usual, your wisdom is unearthing something I guess I already knew."

"Like what, Sam?"

"Thinking about where my most valuable lessons came from, I thought back to some people I used to know on the beach. I haven't thought about any of these guys for years. Compared to our corporate world, I would have to say those guys hailed from a different planet. Their lifestyle was far removed from Wall Street. Yet, I've admired them as much as anyone in my life."

"What raises them to such an enviable position?"

"I guess it was their honesty with themselves. That and they were following a lifestyle they really wanted to live. What struck me about them was they were always upbeat, perpetually having a good time. What made them happy was a good game of volleyball, a sunny day, and joking around with each other. Their lives were pretty simple, really. Unlike many people, they were able to have what they wanted more often than not."

"Sounds like a great bunch to hang around."

"They were. There were plenty of other people on the beach who bitched and moaned about not having this or that. Those people wanted the beach life and a Rolls Royce, too. These guys knew they already had most of what they wanted. Like both of us, knock on wood, they had great family lives. I'd see their kids grow up on the beach. When all is said and done, I think their success was largely due to keeping their needs simple."

In a reflective tone, Art asked, "Have you ever thought about looking any of those guys up?"

"Not really. Although I always knew where I could find them. Right down the beach, hanging out near the volleyball courts at State Beach. Oh, I've run into one or more of them once in awhile at the market or some other place in town. Why do you ask?"

"The reason I ask is it seems to me you've been missing a golden opportunity, Sam. In your pursuit of improving what's important, you want to give yourself the chance to learn from others. If those guys were valuable to you back then, they may still be of value for you today."

"You mean I should seek their advice on mergers and acquisitions?"

Quick as lightning, Art countered with, "You got five bucks on you, Sam?"

Darn. He nailed me. Even though I didn't mean it to be that way, what I said was sarcastic. And, not having the five dollars to ante-up was annoying. What hurt worse was realizing how I had put down some super guys.

"Sorry, Art. I don't have a dime on me. I owe you...and thanks for catching me. What I said was out of line. When you suggested I look those guys up, I'm sure it wasn't for ideas about high finance. I know there must be a good reason you made that suggestion."

"Maybe, and maybe not. All I wanted you to do was consider the thought. When looking for a better way, I feel it is always wise to seek out the ideas of others. There's an old saying I learned from a good friend of mine that goes something like *if the only person you listen to is yourself, you have a fool for a teacher.*'"

What Art was saying made sense. Even when we're too proud to admit it, there are always people who can help improve whatever it is we're trying to improve. Art's a prime example himself. Over the years he's been asked to sit on dozens of boards. Not because they're desperate for warm bodies, but because he's a storehouse of good ideas. Now I know if he's suggesting I seek the ideas of others, he must believe this is good advice for himself, too. I wondered whom he's sought advice from. So I asked.

"Nice question. I'm happy to say I've been pretty lucky in that department. Over the years I've put together a personal board of advisors. Whether you know it or not, you're on the board. You see, this board is an unofficial one. It holds no scheduled meetings. There's no compensation, and no honors associated with being a member. I've picked my board to help me.

Take you, for instance. I've learned a lot from you. Every time I sought your input, something valuable came my way for my efforts. I've assembled a wonderful set of people who are my most treasured resources. What you might find interesting is a couple of them might be described as similar to your locals from the beach—people you wouldn't readily think of as sources of good ideas and advice."

Listening to Art, I had to admit I always saw our relationship as pretty one-sided. He gave me everything from the opportunity to succeed to his own wealth of sound advice. As far as I was concerned, all I ever gave in return was living up to the trust Art had demonstrated in me. Now he tells me I was a member of his board of advisors. I must be smarter than I thought.

"Gee, thanks for the distinction of being on your personal board, Art. If any ideas I've given you have helped a fraction as much as yours have helped me, then I probably earned the honor."

"I'm glad you feel that way. You do deserve a place of honor. If I'm sincere about what I'm preaching here, I ought to look to bright young stars like you for ideas. When you choose to improve those things you are truly committed to, an integral piece is learning from others. The smartest people I've ever met have developed a network of key people. People they can bounce their ideas off of and listen to. People who have the capability of sparking their creativity."

"Is this the role of your informal board of advisors?"

"Precisely. Taking everything I've been given credit for, little do I deserve any star billing. I'd be kidding myself to think the lion's share of what I've implemented was due to personal brilliance. The credit belongs to others. They've shaped my thinking. Improved upon it. Changed it in ways I'd never have achieved alone. And, therein lies their usefulness."

"Could you give me an example?"

"As many as you want. I've learned some little things that have served me well. I've also learned some big things that have immeasurably aided me through life. For instance, probably the biggest and most valuable lesson I ever learned about business was from Frank Grisanti. His ideas formed the basis of the value statement for our company."

"And, who was Grisanti?"

"A successful businessman. At one point in his career he ran a consulting firm. His business was based on four basic principles. He called them his Grisanti Rules:

1. Only do business with people at your level of integrity
2. Only accept work you are fully qualified to perform
3. Know the rules of the business you are working with
4. Don't be a pig"

I had to chuckle. Being able to rattle these off at a moment's notice showed me he'd learned these four rules well. More to the point, Art was a living example of all four. I could also see how they colored the value statement on which Art founded his own business.

"What I'm picking up on is the importance of creating for yourself the circumstances where you can learn from good people. Right?"

"Right! Now, in building a network, it's important to be selective. Everyone won't be of equal service. Some people won't add much to your looking for a better way. Likewise, don't trap yourself into thinking any one person will give you the best advice for everything. That's why you want to have advisors. Notice I use the plural. I said advisors, a cross-section of talent. Look around you. Pick the useful ones, people who are capable of giving you new ways of thinking about things. Create an active idea network. Don't fill it with people who think just like you do. You want to build diversity of thinking."

"Like my old chums from the beach?"

"Like anyone who has a good mind and seems to have a sound perspective on things. Take those guys from the beach. I bet you they could've given some solid advice on what to do about Curt and what to do about the charitable activities he was criticizing. Maybe this surprises you, but I have a gut feeling they would've had some good ideas on these issues. What do you think?"

He was probably right. It doesn't take a corporate career to deal with those problems. What it does take is common sense about human nature. Come to think of it, they probably could have given me some very interesting advice. Some of them were junior high school teachers, and good ones at that. It wasn't such a crazy idea to consider seeking their input. I'd been relying heavily on Art as my mentor. Hmm! Wonder who else I could be talking to?

"I think you're making me feel pretty dumb. My old buddies from the beach certainly have enough experience among them. I haven't considered tapping into their words of wisdom since I was sixteen years old. How could I be so blind?"

Art didn't come to my rescue as he often did. I was fishing for a little don't-be-so-hard-on-yourself consolation that Art was so good at. All I got was silence. If Art was feeling sorry for me or was impressed with my honesty, he was disguising it well. His gaze centered on the sunset.

The sun was low enough to look at directly without any damage. Its lower rim was beginning to press the edge of the horizon. The size and brilliance of this tranquil spectacle almost made me lose my train of thought. Resisting the urge to keep talking, I succumbed to the delicate stillness of nature transitioning from lightness to darkness.

Neither of us spoke during the sun's fleeting descent beneath earth's border. The billowing cumulus clouds were the first to show signs of darkening. The translucent cirrus held longest to their amber hues. Then, in rapid succession, the oranges surrendered to reds, which in turn, conceded to a smokey brown. When the panorama before us had almost subsided, I reverently broke the silence.

"Did you notice how, just as the sun was disappearing, the sky in the east seemed brighter than the sky in the west?"

"I didn't notice it tonight, Sam. I guess I was too riveted on the changes taking place out west. But, I know what you're talking about.

I've noticed it at other times. Speaking of strange illusions, have you ever seen the green flash at sunset?"

"Green what?"

"The green flash. To my understanding, it's a phenomenon that happens rarely, and only in a cloudless sky. The atmospheric conditions have to be just right. When they are, as the sun disappears below the horizon, there occurs a bright green flash. It lasts an instant. Almost like the flash from a camera. Then it's gone. You really have to be at the right place at the right time and looking."

"No, I've never noticed anything like that. Then, again, I didn't know to look. This is the first I've heard of it. Where did you hear about the green flash?"

"Standing on the deck of a cruise ship off Key West. I was watching the sun sink in a cloudless evening sky when a friend I made on the cruise told me about it. He'd seen it once. Somewhere in the South Pacific. I'm still looking forward to my first time."

"Talking about this green flash and the need to be looking for it to see it reminds me of what we were talking about when the sun started setting. I think I have a tendency to get a little single-minded when it comes to looking for a better way. I never once considered talking to anybody about my problem with Curt except you. More importantly, I've never consciously nurtured a set of key people to bounce ideas off of."

"Well, you say you haven't done it consciously. The reality is you have been doing it. You just weren't aware of it."

"What do you mean, Art?"

"Take Curt. You wanted to improve the situation. Sure, you first looked for a better way on your own. When you hit a dead end, what did you do?"

"I asked Curt."

"That's my point. You followed his lead. When you're trying to improve things and are looking for a better way, use the talent around you. Seek out the thinking of others. Include them. Learn from them.

You learned a valuable lesson from Curt himself. He set a great example. Am I right? How are things going with him now?"

"Oh, he's acting much more positively. It's actually contagious. He's been so good-natured about the fines. The progress we've made is really due to the scheme Curt came up with."

"Yes. But I wouldn't underestimate your contribution. You invited his help…and you listened. Two things not so easy for many people. What I'd like to talk about for a couple of minutes is what I think you did to make that situation so successful. Okay?"

"Okay by me!" I wiggled my chair a little deeper in the sand to settle in and listen to what Art was going to say.

"When you're trying to improve things, the bottom line is looking to change things. Without change, you're not improving anything. Before any real change can take place, two steps are crucial: *looking for a better way* and *learning from others*. These actions, in themselves, change nothing. All we're doing here is coming up with ideas. Technically it's called conceptualizing. The only change happening is behind the eyeballs. We're learning. Now, over the years I've come to realize there are better and worse ways to go about formulating ideas."

As he proceeded, I considered my own arbitrary and seemingly aimless way of coming up with new ideas. Sometimes I'm relatively successful. Other times it's like milking granite. I puzzled at what Art might say about how to make this process a little less chaotic.

Art interrupted the perplexity I was having, "You seem to be thinking about something? What is it?"

"I was wondering how to increase my success rate at coming up with new ideas. My track record is too erratic for my liking. I'm hoping you can enlighten me by what you're about to say."

"I like your choice of words. Erratic. This, unfortunately, is the nature of the beast we're talking about here. I haven't learned how to change the fickle disposition of getting good ideas. What I have learned are some good habits to apply to the process."

"Which are?"

"Do you remember what I said when I invited myself to ski with you in Canada last month?"

Strangely enough, I did. On the phone he had said skiing would be a great setting to discuss the new direction our meetings would be taking. I know now this new direction had been a shift from supporting to improving things. Great! I remember what he said. Now what was he driving at? And, why did he bring this up now? What's the connection?

"You said there was a link between skiing, or at least being at the mountain, and the direction our conversation would be heading. I'm puzzled why you're bringing this up now?"

"Bear with me. It will all make sense in a few seconds. Asking another question may help. Why do you ski?"

"Because I love it. It's fun. It's a challenge. It's healthy. It's invigorating. It's outdoors. There are a dozen reasons I like to ski."

"I doesn't takes a PhD to recognize you thoroughly enjoy skiing, right?"

When I nodded, he continued, "It's very important to have fun. Skiing, to you, is pure fun. When you are looking for a better way and involving others in the process, it helps to have fun. Why? When you're having fun, you're bypassing some of the common roadblocks in developing new ideas. These roadblocks include impatience, competitiveness, fear, and eventually lethargy.

Remember, ideas are the first steps to change. For too many people change is not fun at all. They avoid change by remaining comfortable in the status quo. If you want to be flexible and generate ideas, it helps to relax and enjoy the process."

"I'll agree with you there."

"When we'd benefit by being open to new ideas, a natural instinct is to do the exact opposite. It's called idea killing. We censor our own ideas and criticize the ideas of others. On the other hand, when in play, we are truly in a different mode. Our pride is not so much on the line. Then our competitiveness stays healthy and positive. And possibly most important, we become less impatient with ourselves. Or, put another way, more patient. You might say this is when patience and persistence become one and the same."

"What do you mean?"

"I mean we exhibit both patience and persistence. It's called running through the tape. Not letting up at the end of the race. Let me explain what happens under the opposite conditions. Have you ever experienced when you're just about done with a task, a strong desire to move on, to jump to the next task? Not complete the task you're on? Leave it about 95 percent finished?"

I could think of many times. You get so excited about the next step, you find your energy to move on is much greater than your energy to finish.

"The old task is no longer fun. It's work. When you're having fun, there's no strong desire to do something else. There's no pressure to move on. It's easy to stay with what you enjoy."

I could see what he meant. It's like when you're playing golf and having a great time. On those days you hate to see the eighteenth green. You don't want the round to end. You want to keep on playing. This must be the essence of running through the tape as Art calls it. I could think of many other examples, but I found myself focusing on how I felt at this moment.

Art has the gift of hypnotizing me with his words. When I'm with Art, I enjoy his company. Take tonight. I've felt relaxed and comfortable since we plopped on the sand. Yet, now this good feeling seemed heightened even more—as if his words were influencing me on a physical and emotional level even more than the cognitive level.

Leaning back in my chair with my hands clasped behind my neck, I started to make a whole new set of associations. Art had brought back the memory of our skiing. His point was there is a strong connection between looking, learning, and having fun. I started to see some other connections between skiing and what we'd been talking about. Namely, how commitment is also about improving things. I wanted to test my ideas with Art.

Sitting forward in my chair, I said, "Sorry for changing the subject. But, I've thought of some other connections between skiing and the process of improving a situation. Mind if I ask you a question for a change?"

"Be my guest."

"What is the nature of the surface we ski on?"

"Obviously snow…preferably dry powder. What are you driving at?"

"Just that nothing grows on ice. If we limit ourselves to what we already know, we literally freeze our minds. No new ideas have a chance to sprout. To improve, you have to look outside standard thinking. You begin to break with convention."

"Very astute, Sam. I'd say you're making an elemental point. When you're supporting your commitments, you are dealing with what already exists. When you shift to improving things, you are breaking new ground."

"Speaking of ground, there's another connection to be made. There is a connection between the two places where we've discussed looking for a better way and learning from others. Do you know what it is?"

I think this question tickled Art's curiosity. He rubbed his hands together and began to muse over my question. While he was thinking, I sat back and noticed how many stars were now visible in the night sky. I also noticed how riveted I had been on our discussion. For the first time, it hit me how hungry I really was.

While Art reflected on my question, I began to unpack the food basket. Spreading the contents in front of us, I remember I'd never looked at what was in the basket. Now it was so dark, I chuckled to myself that I'd have to taste half of this stuff to know what it was.

As I dished up a little of everything onto two plates, Art quipped, "The mind is what the mind is fed. By the same token, the body is what the body is fed. I'm too hungry to think any more."

We both laughed at the esoteric depths our conversation had reached. With the food spread out, we agreed it was time for supper. While we ate, our conversation drifted to less high-minded and noble ventures. Art handed me a familiar piece of paper as we were cleaning up. I couldn't make it out in the dark, but I knew what it said. I folded it carefully and stuck it in the pocket of my jacket.

The sand was cold on the walk back to our cars. After dumping everything in the trunk, I thanked Art for another enjoyable outing. I asked him where we should meet next month. He told me there were only two more times we would meet. He wanted to pick the next one. I could make the choice of our last setting. With the chill settling in, we didn't dally in the parking lot.

As I climbed into my car, it struck me I hadn't considered these meetings would end someday. Our monthly get-togethers had become so valuable; I didn't want them to stop. Over the last six months, I had come to savor these times. Why did Art say there would be only two more?

Instinctively, I reached in my pocket and pulled out the paper he had given me. Only two spots remained on the page. When Art finished the list, we'd stop getting together. He had said he wanted to make sure I knew what had led him to select me for the job. He obviously felt I did all these things well. As reassuring as this thought was, I had a nagging feeling. After our last two meetings, would he drop out of sight again? I couldn't shake it.

COMMITMENT	
SUPPORT	IMPROVE
Focus on What's Important	Look for a Better Way
Lead by Example	Learn From Others
Reward Success	
Manage Disrespect	

Sitting at the wheel of my car, I looked at the darkened ocean. I could barely make out the waves undulating toward their final resting place on shore. The ever-persistent flow of waves reminded me of a fascinating fact about the human body. Every year the body replaces an amazing 98 percent of its cells. With a body that physically renews itself, I wondered how many of us do the same mentally. How much do we allow our minds to grow? How many times do we afford ourselves the opportunity to learn from others?

At this moment I realized our conversation never returned to the question I asked before supper. Our last two meetings had a physical connection—the connection of being on the edge. When you ski, especially on steep terrain, you realize how close you are to the edge of gravity. The beach is similarly the edge between land and sea, the boundary between what is solid and what is not.

Courage is doing what you are afraid to do.
There can be no courage unless you are afraid.

— Eddie Rickenbacker

Chapter 8

CHALLENGE SUCCESS

Even though the main point from our last meeting was learning from others, I was not doing so well. I hadn't learned anything about our March meeting. This was not due to lack of effort on my part. Art was being genuinely secretive. The only clues I had were to dress casually, and because Art had to make some sort of reservation, the meeting time had been fixed in advance.

Precisely at the appointed time, Art drove up feverishly honking his horn. As I climbed into the front seat, he flashed a devilish smile as we made eye contact. The twinkle in his eye left an unsettling sensation in my stomach. What was in store for us? I had more than an inkling he was up to something I wouldn't approve of. Why else would he be so evasive? Not wanting to prolong my anxiety, I rummaged through a couple of ideas on how I might pry some details out of him. I settled on one of the more polite options.

"Now that you have me captive, how about telling me where we're going."

"In due time...in due time."

Realizing he wasn't going to give me any satisfaction, I began looking for some clues based on the general direction we were heading. A burning curiosity, the driving force behind looking for a better way, helps locate what you are looking for. It can also find things you're not. When I probed Art on this point he had sidestepped the issue, vaguely agreeing with the possibility. I had a sinking feeling I didn't want to reach our destination.

Terror struck the second Art turned on Bundy Avenue. We seemed to be heading for Santa Monica Airport. He knew flying wasn't on my list of enjoyable experiences. I'm passable as a business traveler, as long as I'm riding on a major carrier's wide-body. When it comes to small aircraft, forget it. I'll do just about any song-and-dance necessary to avoid them. I'm sure the dread in my eyes was matched by the trepidation in my voice.

"Excuse me, Art, but you're not heading for Santa Monica Airport, are you? I just want to know whether to bail out now or wait for the next red light."

"No need to panic, Sam. I know you don't like to fly. We are heading for the airport, though. But, before you jump, let me assure you we are not going up in airplane...unless you want to." With that he looked over and said, "Okay?"

I felt better. No need to make an emergency exit at the next light. But, why was he taking me to the airport? What was up his devious sleeve? I gave him a careful look-over as he drove along and noticed a pair of pilot's sunglasses hooked inside his top shirt button. Whatever he was up to, he didn't have a prayer of getting me in a small plane without a good fight. I was willing to follow along with the plan—as long as he stuck to his word about the flying.

Heading into the airport, I realized I was suddenly on foreign ground. I'd never been at this airport. Generally, my feeling about going to small airports rests right up there with teeth extraction. Nestled on the edge of an elevated plateau in West Los Angeles, this airport's like a little village. Unlike LAX, it had a number of different streets crisscrossing the property with buildings carelessly scattered about. Apparently, the place was developed before the concept of a master plan came into vogue.

Art drove through the maze with the assurance of someone who had been here many times before. We wound up parking along the side of a fairly large hangar. Setting the brake, Art exclaimed too gleefully for my liking, "I want to show you something inside."

Unbuckling, I reluctantly left the safe haven afforded by the front seat. Despite my resolve, I knew Art was going to work on me to go flying. There was no other logical explanation for bringing me here. Following him up the single concrete step and through a door of the hangar, it took a moment for my eyes to adjust to the darker interior.

I could make out the dim outline of an airplane as we skirted along one of the walls of the hangar. Most of the light shining in came from a window at the far end of the hangar near the ceiling. Its shape followed the curve of the roofline, clearly showing that the roof of the building formed a shallow arch. The bottom of this window framed the top of a set of accordion-like doors that served as access for airplanes into and out of the hangar. A pencil-thin ray of light showed through the cracks between each door. I counted seven of these skinny beams streaming in as I hastened to keep up.

As we made our way toward the front of the hangar, Art yelled out a hello to an unseen accomplice. Expecting a human response, I jumped when we were greeted by a loud bang. This was followed by a slow, rhythmic creaking as the massive hangar doors directly in front of us rolled open. The gush of light streaming in caused me to divert my eyes over my right shoulder where they rested on the pure white skin of the plane I had spotted when we entered.

I'd never seen anything like it, at least not first-hand. Parked at a slight angle, like a fashion model flashing a sultry pose, it gave off an aura of intrigue. It struck me as some off-the-wall, aviation experiment kept secret under lock and key. My mind raced through a dozen thoughts, all negative. The wings were in the wrong spot. They were way too small for the body. The propellers were mounted backwards. And, what was that apparatus on the nose? The thought holding the firmest grip on my psyche was that this contraption looked remarkably like a hammerhead shark.

As I was giving the plane my jaundiced inspection, Art asked what I thought of her. I really didn't want to communicate how negative I felt. Struggling to come up with something positive, I finally blurted out, "It's so white."

I winced at my bumbling, less-than-clever comment. But, anything else would divulge my true sentiment.

"Just about leaves you speechless, doesn't it…I had the same reaction the first time I laid eyes on her."

If he only knew how dead wrong he was! As he talked, Art moved closer to the fuselage to give the plane a closer look. Caressing the cabin with his hand, he continued, "A pilot friend of mine told me about this beauty a couple of months ago. This is the only one I know of in L.A."

Not really interested in an answer but trying to appear so, I ventured the harmless question, "What kind of plane is it?"

"It's a Piaggio P.180 Avanti. As far as I know, it contains more new aerodynamic design features than any other business turboprop. Looks kind of far-out, doesn't it?"

"You bet it does. Way too far-out for my liking. To be honest with you, Art, this place gives me the creeps. I feel like I'm swimming in a pool with a circling shark. What is that thing on the nose of the plane, anyway?"

"It's a small, fixed-forward wing called a canard. The reason is purely technical…to manage pitch-control. You've probably noticed the main wings are located pretty far aft of the passenger cabin bulkhead. The canard helps with problems created by having such a short distance between the wings and tail."

"I assume all this is supposed to be in the spirit of making improvements. Is that why you wanted to show me this airplane?

"For the most part, yes. The Avanti is the perfect example of what I wanted to talk about today."

"Great! So, now we can go?"

In a voice noticeably calmer than my own, Art responded, "If you're really uncomfortable, I'm willing to leave right now. Before we do, though, I'd like to know one thing. I know you're not a fan of flying. Right now, we're only in a hangar. Is your fear so great it's suffocating your curiosity about such an unusual plane?"

He was right. I was letting my fears take over. All we were doing was looking at a peculiar looking airplane. I guess I was subconsciously protecting myself from some elaborate trick of Art's to get me up in this contraption. I also knew Art's intention to talk about commitment and improving things. We had already discussed looking for a better way and learning from others. I was doing neither of these well since discovering the airport was our destination. I had successfully shut down any curiosity I might have had about the Avanti.

"I'm sorry, Art. I've been so occupied with avoiding any scheme of yours to get me in this thing, I've let my fear replace any real curiosity I might have."

"So, we can stay for little longer and chat?"

"Sure."

"Good. Now we can talk about something really important, something vital to commitment."

Pointing at the Avanti, he continued, "Take this plane as an example. If you are going to improve something, you have to do more than what we've talked about in our last two meetings. The engineers obviously did a marvelous job of looking for a better way.

A key feature in the design of a business aircraft is a spacious cabin. The fundamental problem is providing roominess inside and still being able to fly fast in a cost-effective manner. Doing all three is a real trick. Each goal works against the other two. The process the Avanti engineers went through while looking for a better way and learning I'd say was truly scholarly. Yet, to pull it off, to coax this aircraft off the drawing board and into the sky, required far more than we've discussed so far."

I could feel myself being pulled in. My curiosity was beginning to take a more secure grip. I felt like raising my hand and asking, 'What else do we need to talk about?'

"Let me give you something to think about, Sam. Suppose you were one of the Piaggio engineers. You've come up with the idea to move the wing structure back to avoid eating up precious cabin space. The long fuselage suspended in front of the wings creates a host of new problems to solve. You do your homework and come up with a set of solutions to overcome these problems. What would you do next?"

"I assume the next thing would be to sell my ideas to my fellow engineers. Get my peers to buy into my proposed solution."

"Do you think you might face any resistance?"

"Depends."

"On what?"

"On how different my solutions are from my fellow engineers' current ways of thinking. The more different my new ideas, the more resistance I'd probably face. Assuming my ideas hold merit and I present myself well, I should be able to overcome their resistance with time."

"Maybe. But, most likely, you'd face a steep uphill climb. Take your own experience today. When you first saw the P.180 Avanti sitting here, what was your reaction?"

"Pretty negative. But, that's different. I'm scared of flying. I hate the thought of it in these small planes. These engineers, on the other hand, are working on something they fundamentally like. They're aeronautical engineers and they are designing a new airplane. They would be a lot more predisposed to keep their minds open, receptive, and curious."

"I only partially agree with you. Your resistance basically comes from, as you've said, fear. After all these years there are still many people who, like you, feel the same way Lord Kelvin did in 1899. As president of Britain's prestigious Royal Society, he made the untimely pronouncement that heavier-than-air flying machines were impossible. If your mind gravitates toward this kind of thinking, it's easy to be afraid."

"You bet it is. With the difficulties of keeping an airplane aloft—defying gravity—the natural thing is to think flying is unnatural."

"Speaking of what's natural, did it ever occur to you that our aeronautical engineers can be equally closed and unreceptive? Their reaction, instead of coming from lack of knowledge, comes from having too much of it. They are the experts.

As experts, they have amassed a huge amount of knowledge and understanding. This accumulated expertise eventually can solidify—or maybe a better word is petrify—into a set of assumptions. Any new idea conflicting with their well-grounded assumptions and beliefs will receive a reaction just like the one you had when we drove to the airport. When the foundations of their assumptions are shaken, they are likely to discard any curiosity they might naturally have and put blinders on instead."

I knew what he was talking about. Often when I work with "the experts" on some business issue, they tended to act a lot more dogmatic and inflexible in their thinking than nonexperts. After reaching this conclusion, I suddenly found myself examining the P.180 with fresher eyes.

Looking over the plane, I mentioned, "I guess those who genuinely make improvements are the ones who can stretch their imagination and challenge their own well-grounded assumptions and expectations. The engineers on this plane seem to have been pretty good at challenging traditional thinking. What can and might be done. Every part of this plane seems to have features I haven't seen on other airplanes."

"For having an untrained eye, Sam, you're pretty perceptive. We could walk up one side and down the other and I could tell you about refinements that solve specific problems created by a solution to other problems. The Avanti really is an elegant system, a stream of innovations. When the engineers were finished, they succeeded in creating an aerodynamic design with remarkably low-drag properties."

"Do you mean *drag* the same way we use it in cycling?"

"Pretty much the same. What I mean is this plane has less resistance when it moves through the air. It stays aloft easier. With the aerodynamics incorporated in the design, the P. 180 floats and glides easier. Think of it more closely resembling the properties of a feather than a rock."

Intruding on our privacy, a young man with a tool kit sauntered around the corner and through the hangar doors. When Art spotted him, the young man waved with his free hand, "Good to see you, Mr. Brunsing."

It was obvious they knew each other when Art returned the greeting with, "Hi, James." As James climbed into the open hatch of the P.180 he asked if we wanted to have a look around inside.

Art looked at me, clearly indicating it was my call. Since I was feeling more comfortable, I welcomed the opportunity to poke around. I wanted to see just how spacious the cabin really was. Leading the way, I headed for the open hatch on the left side of the cabin. Being right next to the fuselage, I noticed how low and sleek the plane was. The looks of the P.180 were beginning to grow on me. It started to look more like a Lamborghini than a hammerhead. Yet, I still felt a little hesitant about actually climbing inside.

Once inside, my first comment was, "Not as roomy as a 747."

As soon as I said it, I remembered our little bet about making sarcastic remarks. I wondered if Art would remember. I waited for him to give me another five dollar fine. As it turned out, he didn't pick up on my remark. Or he didn't choose to. Instead, he motioned to one of the seats and invited me to sit, "Let's check out the leg room."

The seat was very comfortable. Settling in, I decided to delve into our real purpose for coming here today.

"I'm beginning to see why you brought me here. We both know we're talking about commitment to improve. I'm sure you alluded to the next key step in the process when you asked me what I would do if I were an engineer with a new idea about the design of this plane. If I'm following you right, you steered me to the possibility of facing resistance to my ideas. Is that right?"

"That's correct."

"If my logic holds, the next step to improvement is unfreezing resistance to new ways of looking at things. Am I on the right track?"

"Given our location, I'd say you're in the right hangar. So, how would you, using your metaphor, unfreeze people?"

I had to think about this one before answering. Based upon all we've talked about, I knew I'd like to find a positive way if possible. But how? Shaking people out of their customary way of thinking or acting seemed a tall order, at least if you're going to keep it positive. Looking at my own behavior this afternoon, I could attest to the difficulty. Sitting in the cabin of a small airplane, while a young mechanic swapped parts in the cockpit was no picnic on the beach. How in the world did I get in here anyway?

"This is a hard question to answer, Art. What I'm coming up with is a bit scanty. One thing I've learned from you is to persist in finding a positive way. When it comes to helping people see things in a whole new light, I'm coming up short on the how-tos. Maybe I'm part of the problem. When I look at myself today, I've got to say I've set a lousy example up till now."

"I'd say you were predictable. Both with your initial resistance and then your shift to a more positive viewpoint."

James stuck his head in the cabin to say he was finished. Excusing himself, he passed through the hatch leaving us alone in the Avanti. This gave me a moment to think about what Art just said. How in the world could he consider my behavior positive? I've been a far greater example of someone resisting than someone embracing something new. If Art saw things differently, I figured he might as well explain himself.

"How so? In what ways have I been a good example?"

"Let me answer that in the cockpit." Without any hesitation he stood up and walked toward the front of the plane. For a moment I sat there contemplating his invitation to follow. Grudgingly, I put both hands on the armrests and pushed myself up. Art was already sitting in the pilot's seat. Sensing I was coming, he patted the seat next to his, motioning for me to sit down.

Before I finished reclining in the chair, Art asked, "Why did you follow?"

I knew what he was up to. "I know what you're driving at…I've been willing to follow you this far. Maybe I am here sitting in the cockpit of a small plane, but, my attitude remains rather negative. If I've come across as willing, let me tell you, inside I'm real iffy. Every move's been a painful experience, filled with a heavy dose of vacillation."

"Do you think real change is ever any different?"

"I guess not."

"I *know* not…Look, I knew this experience today wasn't going to be pleasant for you. This is no family ski trip or watching a beautiful sunset on the beach. I knew you weren't going to have fun today. You were really closed-minded about coming to the airport once you found out where we were going. Unless I'm dead wrong, you're certainly more open to the idea now. You've been experiencing a change. I'm not saying it's a big change. I'm not saying it's a small one, either. Let's not underestimate what I've put you through."

He was right about that. Noticing your own heartbeat without feeling for your pulse is a sure sign things are on the stressful side.

"Sam, do you remember what I did this afternoon that started you in a more positive direction?"

"I've been trying to tell you—I haven't been all that positive."

"Sure you have. Don't equate enjoyment or fun as prerequisites for acting positively. One of the most positive experiences is learning something new. Challenging assumptions and expectations that are no longer useful is positive. It often takes some time to feel it. Nonetheless, with hindsight, it's often described as one of life's most valuable experiences…Now, let me ask you again, do you remember what I did that started you in a more positive direction today?"

"Art, I feel like I've been through the wringer. I haven't the foggiest idea what you did to trigger the change in me. I do feel different now. But, you're going to have to help me out."

"Be happy to, Sam. What I did was really quite simple. I gave you a challenge…I'm sure you're trying to figure out what that challenge was and when I did it."

"Sure am."

"Only a few minutes after you saw this plane you were ready to throw in the towel and go home. First, I acknowledged your fear. Then I challenged you. I asked if your fear was stifling your curiosity. That's all it took to hook you. Knowing you have a curious nature, I knew what you'd do. You prefer to think of yourself more as someone with a sense of adventure and inquisitiveness than someone who is cowardly or doesn't give a damn."

The bum was right. He had sucker-punched me. Before I knew what hit me, Art had challenged me to be curious. I took the bait without blinking an eye. So, that's how he did it, with a challenge.

"I have to admit it worked. I swallowed your challenge like a hungry trout would a fat worm. My curiosity about what you were up to and what I didn't know diverted me from my fears."

"And, that's how I help someone start the process of change. I challenge 'em. The important thing to remember is that the challenge has to be a positive one."

"One filled with enchantment."

"I like that! Yes. A good challenge has a real sense of mystery to it. You have to want to know how things will turn out and care about playing a part in making it happen."

"Art, I'd have to add that any challenge you give someone has to be tempered with a sense of reality. The challenge has to be realistic."

"Without a doubt. Remember, I never challenged you to actually fly in this plane. I also didn't challenge you not to be afraid. Both of those challenges would be unrealistic in my eyes."

"Instead you challenged me to live up to something I believe about myself. I believe in looking for a better way and the value of learning. The challenge was to live up to those beliefs."

"Let's not forget I selected you as my successor because you already possess those qualities."

What Art said had an interesting effect on me. All of a sudden I made a stronger connection to something I had said in passing a little while earlier. The tough part about commitment is we have to be ever vigilant about challenging ourselves. We have to be humble about what we know and don't know.

"I guess if I were really good today, I would have challenged myself. I wouldn't have had to wait for you to do it for me."

"That's an excellent observation. What I want to get across today is the power of an accepted challenge. The challenge can come from within. It doesn't have to come from someone else. If commitment includes this striving to improve, you become willing to challenge almost anything. If I were going to summarize today's conversation I'd call it...*challenging current expectations*."

"Art, I just had a thought. It's becoming increasingly clear to me that we all have to challenge our own thinking, not just the thinking of others. Wouldn't challenging ourselves be a first step toward looking for a better way and seeking out those we can learn from?"

"Perfecto! When personally looking for a better way, learning from others, and challenging current expectations, all three are closely interwoven. From a personal standpoint, challenging yourself and your expectations might actually occur as a first step to looking for a better way. There is no sequence etched in stone on how we make improvements. What I do know is doing all three—looking, learning, and challenging—is part of the process."

"You know, Art, I never thought too much about it before, but it's no accident the word *challenge* is part of your vocabulary."

"I choose to use it often. Do not underestimate the power of this word. From my own observation, I found that the word *challenge* is used frequently by effective leaders. Why? Because it takes the fast lane to the heart of human motivation."

"What do you mean *to the heart?*"

"One of the most basic human needs is mastery. Another way of saying it is a sense of competence. We all crave to be masters of our surroundings."

"Success is a great aphrodisiac."

"I agree. Challenge offers the promise of a better future. The consummate leaders take advantage of our need to strive for mastery. They challenge their own success and the success of others."

"I see your point. When you initially take on a challenge, there's almost an involuntary surge of mastery. Even when there is a strong sense of apprehension, there's also an anticipation, a sense of faith you're going to succeed."

"Sure, I think such feelings are universal. Remember, we're talking about a challenge to improve. We're talking about something we're committed to. We're not talking about lowering the bar. We're talking about raising it, moving to a higher level. Doing something better than it has been done before."

Leaning forward and motioning to our somewhat cramped quarters Art said, "Sam, I chose to meet in this airplane. It represents state-of-the-art aeronautical design, at least as we now speak. Tomorrow it will be nothing but a footnote in the history books. That's the nature of things. Progress is forged from commitment."

Sitting back, Art folded his hands behind his head. He looked content. I could sense he had achieved what he wanted from our meeting today. Then, he turned towards me and said, "Where we meet next time is your choice."

"Thanks. I'd love to return the pleasure. Before I do, I'd like to take today's discussion to heart. Can I challenge an assumption I've had about our meetings?"

"Sure."

"I've felt it was appropriate to wait until we actually met to find out the particular point you wanted to discuss. I'm going to challenge that by asking if I can find out ahead of time what we'll be talking about next?"

"I think it's perfectly fine to know ahead of time. For all I know, it may even be better to know in advance. In our final meeting, I want to discuss the toughest thing we'll talk about in all our meetings."

Wonder what he meant by that? Everything we'd talked about seemed to be both tough and easy. Easy in that the principles were generally simple. Difficult in that it's hard to persist and faithfully use them. As I was thinking, Art gave me the answer.

"Risk Making Changes. That is what we'll be talking about. To really make improvements, the last step after you've looked, learned, and challenged yourself and others, is actually taking the risk and making a change."

I should have known this would be the end of it all. When you think about it, we could have started with taking risks. If you're going to improve on anything, you're going to have to do something new. So risk making changes is it? That gave me a great idea for where we should meet for our final encounter. This place is certainly different from where we've been meeting. Yet, it would be perfect.

"Thanks a million for letting me know what we'll be talking about. It helps me sort out where we should meet. Since we are going to talk about *risk making changes*, and in light of the fact we met under these circumstances," I motioned around the cabin of the airplane, "I'm going to challenge your expectations a little."

"I don't know what you mean, Sam."

"Ah! The shoe's on the other foot this time! The only thing you need to know right now is make sure your and your wife's passports are up to date."

"Sounds intriguing. I'll check first thing when I get home." After a moment's reflection, Art continued, "I think we've covered a lot of ground this afternoon. How about a little dinner?"

As we started out the hatch, I offhandedly asked, "Did you rent this thing with the idea we'd actually take her up?"

"Does it matter?"

Purposefully I avoided an answer. Art hesitated, waiting for my reply. Then shrugging his shoulders, he stepped out the hatch. We were about a dozen steps from the plane when I asked, "Do you have the keys?"

As he rummaged through his pants pockets looking for the keys, I said, "Sometimes it's good to quicken the old pulse."

With the same twinkle in his eye I saw when we first made eye contact this afternoon, he pulled out the set of keys and dangled them enticingly in front of me. Not a word was spoken. The eye contact was enough. We were off.

Anyone who has had a bull by the tail knows five
or six things more than someone who hasn't.

— Mark Twain

Chapter 9

BE DISRESPECTFUL

Today seemed different. When the captain released the brakes and accelerated down the runway, he also seemed to unleash a latent conflict going on inside me. With the sudden acceleration of the huge jet engines, part of me flooded with a sweeping sense of anticipation. For once, I wanted to take off. I wanted a chance to put all I've learned to work. There was no way to do this without getting home.

There was this other feeling, though. Deep inside, I was filling sandbags. Somewhere in an almost inaccessible location, I was trying to stem my flood of excitement. My head was ready to leave. My heart wasn't. I really didn't want to say goodbye to Art. I had a strong feeling I'd never see him again.

As we climbed away from Milan and set our course for California, I looked off toward the southern horizon. I knew it was pointless, but in my imagination I was trying to get one last glimpse of Florence. The early morning haze gave the landscape an even softer appearance than normal. Vainly, I tried to pierce the mist. Even though I knew it was impossible to see the towers rising above the rooftops of the palazzos, I knew I'd feel better trying.

Fighting weariness, I stared out the window. I was determined to fix on the point where Florence would be on the horizon. When this imaginary spot drifted out of sight behind the tail section, I almost involuntarily closed my eyes. I could feel the adrenalin leaving my body. Reaching for the button to recline my seat, a thought jolted me out of my enveloping cocoon.

What if I went to sleep and woke up unable to remember what Art and I talked about? Our five days were already beginning to take on a dream-like quality. What if I couldn't rekindle my fleeting memory? Instead of focusing on my return home, I found myself in reflection. I wish I could start the week over again. The excitement, the charm of the city, the long strolls, the meals, and especially our conversations were all worth a second experience.

My mind raced backwards, far past Florence. During the past eight months, Art had shown me what he meant by commitment. He delivered on his initial promise. Now I have a good sense of what he saw in me and what he wanted in a replacement. I realized that instead of looking back, the right thing to do was move forward.

It was time to sit, relax, and enjoy the trip back to the States. Noticing Kris was already drifting off to sleep, I shut my own eyes. Exhausted as I was, a light, fitful sleep was the best I could attain. My subconscious wandered back to our week in Florence. We spent a good part of the time talking about risk taking. Out of everything Art had said during our many meetings, this is probably where I'd rate myself the highest. It's one thing I've always prided myself in doing exceptionally well. I remember a compliment Art once gave me.

He said, "You always make it look so easy, like an Englishman doing Shakespeare."

As good as I am, though, Art was the consummate risk-taker. He was always trying out new ideas. Sure, he had his setbacks. Yet, he always seemed to rebound unscathed from the experience.

Looking out the window, I thought about the choice of Florence as the setting for our last discussion. My main motive was to pick a spot that would ensure a longer visit than just one afternoon. I also saw Art as a modern day Renaissance man. What better place to end our meetings than the cradle of the Italian Renaissance?

After a day-and-a-half with our spouses, Art and I took a long walk alone for the first time. We slowly wandered through the old section of the city until we stumbled upon the Arno. Crossing the river at Ponte Santa Trinita, we stopped at one of the supporting piers. From the low wall of the bridge, we captured an unobstructed view of the famed Ponte Vecchio.

I suggested we jump the low wall and sit on the pier for awhile. The distance we had to jump was by no means difficult. The return climb up was, however, a different situation. The thought of getting back to the street side of the wall might stop the hesitant. As usual, this didn't apply to Art. He was game. So, we scaled the wall and jumped onto a triangle of concrete protruding from the bridge.

Using the outer wall of the bridge as our backrest, we wiled away the good part of an hour looking at the Ponte Vecchio while discussing the importance attitude has in taking risks. Malcolm Forbes best described my fundamental attitude: *Failure is success if we learn from it.* I remembered Art's comment on this quote.

He said, "Not taking a risk is giving up an opportunity to learn something. The most productive state of mind is one that views the real risk as not taking any."

We both agreed that any time you take a risk you give yourself an opportunity to surpass yourself.

As Art said, "Every risk is a fresh start. It goes without saying that you can't improve your batting average if you don't get up to bat. Commitment means continually putting yourself up to the plate. What can make taking the challenge so compelling are the possibilities—what you might be able to accomplish if you pull it off. I know that this is what I always found so invigorating about taking risks."

Through much of the afternoon we swapped stories of people who seemed to demonstrate risk-taking with a flair for greatness. Art talked about Seymour Cray, the father of supercomputers. Most computer scientists alive today have never experienced a time when the world's fastest computer was other than a Cray design. His passion for continually building the fastest machine had been realized over a number of decades.

A story attributed to Cray is that he builds a new sailboat by hand every year. Once finished, he burns it to the ground. The reason is to avoid becoming a prisoner to his prior designs when he once again picks up this task. He wants a fresh start each year.

As Art talked, I noticed the afternoon rowers from the local boathouse maneuvering their single sculls up and down the river. Some of the rowers took a leisurely lap or two. Others worked out long and strenuously. All of them eventually returned to the dock. Some seemed prisoners to a time schedule not of their choosing. Others who stayed longer fell prisoner to exhaustion, albeit also by choice.

Our discussion evolved into talking about the courage it must take to continually push away from safe waters into uncharted ones. Many people struggle with the thought of taking risks and pushing the limits. Risks leave them exhausted, wrung out, emotionally drained. They think risk-taking is like a kamikaze mission where success means diving your plane down the smokestack of an enemy's battleship. Given I was presently at about 37,000 feet, this sobering thought broke my slumber.

Due to the length of time I studied her beautiful shape, the Ponte Vecchio stayed clearly imprinted in my mind, even awake. During World War II, the Germans destroyed all bridges crossing the Arno except the Ponte Vecchio. It alone survived the chaos of that war. Funny how I didn't think about it before. The Ponte Vecchio, this magnificent backdrop to our conversation, was an analogy for what we had talked about. We focused on a person's attitude toward risk. One's state of mind really is the bridge between our natural resistance to an unknown future and our willingness to venture out and take risks to attain what we want from that future.

When I think about the state of mind of risk-takers, a higher degree of innate optimism has little to do with their ability to take chances. In my experience, their attitude is the result of a different vision. They simply see a richer variety of useful outcomes from taking risks than those of a more timid sort. Behind the right state of mind is a simple belief that you learn something of value when you take a risk. This learning will add to the likelihood of success when undertaking future risks. It seems that taking risks is a necessary step to building risk-taking skills.

I remember distinctly Art's last point of the afternoon as we walked back to our *pensione*. He summarized what the right attitude toward risk-taking meant to him.

"A lifelong devotion to trial, experience, learning, and change is the ultimate test of commitment. Notice I didn't say trial and error. Error doesn't have to be part of the equation."

It seemed fitting to me that Art would eliminate the word *error* from his philosophy of risk-taking. I recall a feeling of nostalgia growing within me that second evening in Florence. As this sentiment grew, I knew I wanted to give Art something of lasting remembrance.

Later that night as I strolled back to the *pensione* with Kris, I played around with a saying I'd heard attributed to different people. It had to do with persistence. The next day we went to a local craftsperson and had her engrave my enhanced version of this quote on leather. Once finished, she stretched it on a canvas and framed it in a beautiful leather frame.

The next time Art and I had a few hours alone, I suggested we walk up to the Piazzale Michelangelo where we could get a view of the entire city. Art suggested another option. Whenever I brought up visiting Piazzale Michelangelo, he'd always suggest we hold off until later. The next day we wound up spending a good deal of time wandering through the Bobili Gardens.

In a classic Italian garden built prior to the nineteenth century, not everything is revealed at once. As opposed to one big garden, there are many smaller gardens. Each unveils its own surprises. The vistas found along the garden paths unfold in both familiar and unfamiliar patterns. Obviously, I felt there was a reason Art steered us through the Pitti Palace to these impressive grounds behind. Stopping by the first bed of budding flowers, Art commented that gardeners, by nature, were optimists.

He talked about how planting a seed does not ensure a successful plant. What makes a good gardener is an eye for the future, patience, and a willingness to do what it takes to prepare the soil for growth. A knowledgeable gardener envisions what the garden will look like before it has a chance to grow. The same is true of any effective risk-taker. It all starts with sound preparation.

"What do you do to prepare yourself for taking risks?"

My answer pleased Art immensely.

I said, "If you've looked diligently for a better way, if you've learned from the right people, and if you've challenged current expectations appropriately, then you'll be adequately prepared."

Somewhere along the way, I had realized we had been talking about preparing for risk-taking ever since our ski trip to Canada. That was when we started discussing how to improve things. After giving this rather uncomplicated answer, I went on to explain how I felt proper preparation was accomplished. Mostly it was the result of unglamorous hard work: working to anticipate consequences, developing strategies to deal with likely contingencies, determining how to learn from mistakes if they happen, and planning how to gather information so you can learn quickly.

I remember Art's response to this. He mused, "A person who won't assess an upcoming risk has no advantage over the person who can't."

As we ascended a steep path lined with tall cypress we swapped stories of the risks we had taken in business. We both concluded that most of the risks leading to the greatest return for the company were not of the "bet the farm" variety. None could be called revolutionary. Yet, a common characteristic among them was a genuine *disrespect* for current ways of doing things.

Hitting the crest of the path, you could get a partial glimpse of the city skyline. Florence was a monument to violating the status quo. A truly extraordinary deposit for the arts and sciences, the treasures created by the inhabitants of this city have influenced the way we all see the world.

As the poet, William Blake, so eloquently stated, *Execution is the chariot of genius.* What is publicly displayed throughout Florence is a testimonial to Blake's wisdom. The care and dedication behind these masterpieces is evident centuries later. Strolling through the Uffizi, one of the most select picture galleries in the world, you witness firsthand the value of execution.

Almost everyone aspires to greatness. What makes those who achieve it different from the rest is their willingness to pay the price for success. This price is a willingness to rigorously prepare, practice, rehearse, do whatever it takes to be ready. So, when it comes time to execute, it's done flawlessly. The odds are then stacked in their favor.

Having the right attitude and carefully laying the groundwork through planning only pay off if you execute risks energetically and well. Going after what you want is the bottom line. Maybe it's the most important part. Personally, I hold dearly to what President Teddy Roosevelt said about the strong man who stumbles compared to the critic.

He said something like, *The credit belongs to the man marred by dust and sweat and blood in the arena who strives valiantly; who errs and comes up short, time and time again; who knows great enthusiasm; and who devotes himself to a worthy cause. At best, he knows the triumph of high achievement. At worst, if he fails, at least fails while daring greatly. His place shall never be with those cold and timid souls who know neither victory nor defeat.*

For myself, I've always preferred to be in the ring, not the grand-stands. Nothing pleased me more then when Art said I wasn't afraid to take a big step if one was called for.

With his usual flair, he pointed out, "You can't cross a chasm in two small jumps. When you go for it, you have to go 100 percent."

The last point we talked about on our walk through the gardens was keeping the stakes reasonable. No do-or-die scenarios. When Art asked how I kept risks under control, I fell back on one thing I've always insisted on with my people when they wanted to try something new. I'd make sure we built in feedback mechanisms. This allowed us to learn quickly.

Art laughed when I told him my pet saying when I instructed my coworkers on building in feedback loops: "In the land of the blind, the one-eyed man is king." You may not know it all, but if you know more than the next guy, you're in good shape.

The gentle tap on my shoulder made me realize I'd been dozing. I looked up to see a flight attendant smiling down at me. She asked if I wanted the meal service. Mentioning she had let me sleep through breakfast, she was worried I wouldn't want to miss another meal. Upon hearing I'd missed breakfast, my stomach instantly grew ravenous. Noticing the name on her apron, I responded, "Well, Jessica, do you have an Italian chef on board?"

Jessica's smile widened as she said, "What we lack in fine Italian cuisine we'll try to make up in service."

"Fine. I'm famished. I'd love to eat."

Waiting for the meal service, and trying to ignore my growling belly, I thought back to another pastime we engaged in besides walking around Florence, namely eating. In true Italian fashion, we would spend the good part of an hour simply consuming a couple of cappuccinos and a pastry. Most of the time we would sit outside watching the crowds navigate the city. One of my favorite spots was in the Piazza della Signoria near the Palazzo Vecchio. Close to the Uffizi Gallery, one could always experience the excitement of hordes of people scurrying from one destination to another.

The world seemed split between those hustling about and those luxuriating over the local food and drink. In the small restaurants surrounding the square, the people have a different agenda. One day when the four of us were seated outside, Art with a glass of Tuscan Chianti in hand made a comment that stuck with me.

Motioning to the people scurrying across the Piazza, he said, "With all the excitement, it's easy to get caught up in the moment. I love their spirit. I tip my glass to them. Then again, it's just as good and valuable a time when you should sit back and reflect."

We talked about the importance of reviewing risks, whether in business or elsewhere in life. Great value exists in finding and using all the feedback you can get your hands on. When taking a risk, it is advisable to consciously debrief what you're doing. What went right? What didn't? What are the next steps? How do you move forward? Some people debrief their failures. Many others won't. They are unwilling to put up with the pain. They just move on without really learning anything.

The astute risk-takers work just as hard at learning why they succeeded. They debrief their victories as diligently as their defeats. They're curious about all outcomes, good or bad. Probably the most famous American example of this is Thomas Edison. He was always ready to learn.

There is a saying about him: he knew 1,800 ways not to build a light bulb. Here, in Florence, his counterpart was undoubtedly Leonardo da Vinci. Like Edison, Leonardo saw possibilities the rest of us were blind to. He was the first to recognize that the human eye was a simple receptor. He didn't go along with the commonly held belief that the eye was an elaborate emitter which bounced rays off objects in order to see them. An incredible 150 years before Galileo, da Vinci correctly identified the earth as revolving around the sun.

Men like da Vinci and Edison, who lived in such different circumstances, must have had one thing in common. They had immense courage. The kind of courage needed to push far ahead of accepted thinking. Winston Churchill said it best: *Courage is the finest of human qualities because it guarantees all the others.* If you have the courage to take risks, you will live up to the toughest of commitments.

Having grown up in the United States and finding myself lounging around in a square like the Piazza Signoria, I found the past and the present began to blur. Old and new seemed to blend together so naturally. Art posed an interesting challenge one evening in Florence. He suggested we both try to summarize what we had talked about over the past eight months in a single word. We would each think about it over the next couple of days and share our ideas before we went home.

Art and Marilyn went on an overnight trip to Siena. Kris and I took a more restful approach. We meandered the streets. Window shopping, finding a new *ristorante*, or simply absorbing the view from a choice spot is how we filled our days. Upon their return to Florence, I gave Art the quotation I had framed for him. Unwrapping my gift, Art's face lit up with a wide smile. He let out an ever-so-small chuckle.

COMMITMENT

Commitment is practicing one's beliefs.

Nothing in the world can take the place of commitment.

Talent will not:
Nothing is more common than an unsuccessful person with talent.

Genius will not:
Unrewarded genius is almost a proverb.

Education will not:
The world is full of educated derelicts.

Commitment, persistence with a purpose, is omnipotent.

I asked him what he found funny. He brushed my question aside without really answering. With genuineness in his voice, he thanked me for my thoughtfulness and said the quotation would hang in a place of honor in his study. This simple gift meant the world to him. I wished I could do more. There's no way I could ever pay Art back for all he's done for me.

We started talking about the one word describing the essence of what we had talked about over the past months. I remembered all our conversation as if we were still having them.

I asked Art to think back to our first meeting when we discussed *focusing on what's important*. I reminded him of how I asked for his personal list of what he considered most important. At the time I made this request, I really had an urgent desire to understand. I wanted to discover why Art had been so successful.

I know now, looking back, he wasn't going to satisfy my curiosity immediately. What did come out of that first conversation was a nice list to help keep me focused—Customers, Results, People, Company, and Values. I summarized the value that list had on me concluding with,

"My own list is serving me exceptionally well."

"So, what did you do to live up to those commitments?" For instance, what did you do for our *customers?*"

"For our customers I required myself to make weekly calls on at least two customers I had not seen in the past year—a minimum of one hundred customers a year. I also personally sat at our customer service hot line one hour per week at unscheduled times."

"Both excellent ways to get unfiltered information from customers. How about your *people* commitment? What did you do there?"

"For my commitment to people, I decided to *personally find* at least one employee per week who deserved recognition and write him or her a personal thank you note. Also, I either kicked off or closed at least two sessions we were running at the management development center each month."

Listening thoughtfully, Art added: "This allowed you to show that training and development were important to you. That's a super idea. Just great! Before I lose the thought, I want to go back to your first action. What did you mean when you said you personally found people to write a thank you note to?"

"I wanted a way to ensure I'd get out and talk with our employees. I made it a ritual. I followed the simple motto: *walk the halls*. Whenever the opportunity arose, I'd stop by an employee's work area. This helped me to interact with people firsthand. It also helped me see the dedication and care a lot of our employees take executing their jobs. This was much more valuable than having someone on the staff find people for me to reward."

"I like the personal touch, Sam. It means a whole lot to people."

"Yes, it does. And, what I've described leads to the one word I came up with to summarize our discussions on commitment."

"And, what's that?"

"*Habit!*"

"Interesting choice...go on."

"Habit is what we've been talking about ever since our first conversation. I feel you picked me to be your successor because I already possessed *the habits* you considered important. Habits are those instinctive, ingrained, everyday actions. They don't require conscious, deliberate thought to do. The best way of putting into practice the various principles of commitment we have discussed is making them habits."

"I'd have to agree with you there."

"When I was thinking about our little challenge to come up with a summary word, the one I kept coming up with was *habit*. It's kind of funny, but when I first thought about habits, bad habits came to mind. Even though bad habits seem to form naturally and good habits seem to require constant attention and practice before becoming second nature, to me, the successful incorporation of what we've talked about over these months lies in forming appropriate habits. That's what I forced myself to do with what I learned from you; I made it such a part of me I wouldn't have to think about it."

"Excellent word to pick, Sam. One thing I've learned along the way myself is that true mastery of the principles we've talked about only comes from relentless effort."

"I know what you mean. Building a habit takes awhile. The payoff is good habits work for you 100 percent of the time, even when you're not running at 100 percent yourself. A good habit keeps you from falling into the trap of being too busy to do what's right. And, habits don't require memory. You do them without thinking."

"Yes, it's only hard to do the right thing until it becomes a habit."

The voice of the aircraft captain announcing our landing approach to L.A. startled me out of my slumber. I couldn't believe we were almost home. How long had I been sleeping? Someday all overseas travel will be as quick as this flight felt. For me, this trip was a treat. I wasn't used to feeling at ease on airplanes. In fact, this was the first time I'd ever slept so soundly while in flight. Maybe I'm more relaxed now.

Checking my belt, I looked out the window. I tried to fix our location. The dry Southern California desert was a stark contrast to the Italian landscape we had left a dozen hours earlier. Yet, it was nice to see familiar terrain. I began preparing for our arrival.

First, I squeezed back into my shoes. It's strange how feet can swell so much. Then I started packing my loose personal effects into my carry-on. When the plane rolled slightly from side to side as it decelerated to landing speed, I instantly remembered the rest of my last conversation with Art at the Piazzale Michelangelo.

Art's summary word for all we talked about regarding commitment was *balance*. As the reasons unfolded behind his selection of me, I marveled at the subtlety and depth of his decision-making.

"Balance is the key," he said. "Commitment, to be genuine, endures. It's long-term. That's why balance is so important. A physical analogy makes my point. The best way to conserve your energy is through balance. Being out of balance uses lots of energy. The simple act of standing demonstrates what I mean. When properly balanced, you can stand for a long, long time. When off balance, you tire easily. The same can be said for commitment. Do you see how this applies?"

I did, and responded, "I see it applying to the supporting and improving behaviors. It's too easy to make one an exclusive activity. For instance, you can fall in love with your current level of success. Then, you fall into the trap of restricting yourself to only supporting your successes. You wind up getting stale.

In contrast, when you catch the fever of moving to the next level, when you have that strong desire to make improvements, you can pursue your goal with remarkable tunnel vision. You often wind up forgetting to support what you've already accomplished. From the perspective you've given me, I feel it's crucial to keep these two activities in balance."

"I'm delighted to hear you say it. I see you've connected with commitment at its most fundamental level."

"And, what level is that, Art?"

"What I'm referring to is the behavioral level. To me this is the most important place to understand commitment. This level of understanding is tied to action, to an understanding rooted in behavior. The world is full of people who intellectually possess knowledge. They have a good understanding of commitment at the cerebral level. But, far too many of them never translate this understanding into real action.

When you chose *habit* to summarize our discussions, you were also personalizing our discussions down to the level of your actions. The most basic level of *balance* is keeping your supporting and improving behaviors in balance, making this a habit. Achieving this equilibrium is the foundation for balancing everything else."

Art went on to describe other levels of balance. He pointed out that *balance* also is needed in our commitments to customers, results, people, and the company. These key concepts become the pillars that support long-term profitability and a reputation for excellence. Sacrificing any one of these commitments means the whole dynamic falls off balance.

The last balance point Art mentioned is exactly what I would have expected from him. The importance of balancing commitment to our customers, results, people, and the organization with our values. When each commitment is acted upon in a way consistent with our basic beliefs, everything clicks. With balance all these key elements fit together easily.

The nudge Kris gave me jolted me out of my daydream. It was our turn to go through customs. With nothing to declare—except maybe my deeper understanding of commitment—getting through LAX was easy. Arriving home, I saw the mail neatly sorted and stacked on the buffet. It's always nice to know someone you trust has been watching the house and the kids for you. Dropping my bags inside the door, I noticed a single airmail package underneath a pile of magazines.

Picking it up, I saw the Italian postage. What had Art done? How could he have sent it here so quickly? Tearing off the wrapping, I forgot these questions in my eagerness to get at the contents.

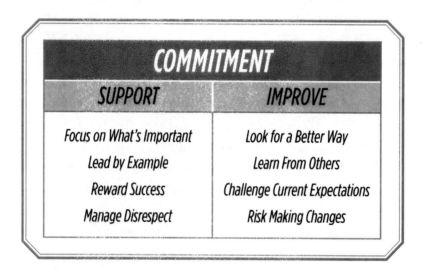

COMMITMENT	
SUPPORT	IMPROVE
Focus on What's Important	Look for a Better Way
Lead by Example	Learn From Others
Reward Success	Challenge Current Expectations
Manage Disrespect	Risk Making Changes

A small note accompanied a framed parchment:

> *Hope you enjoyed the trip to Florence as much as I did. Knowing how you always wanted to keep track of what we talked about, I thought you'd like the final list. Consider this a token of my appreciation for listening to me and what I believe in.*

I had to laugh as I looked at the frame. Now I know what Art chuckled about when I gave him his gift back in Florence. We had virtually the same idea. No wonder he had that funny, little look on his face when I gave him my present. It was a comforting thought that possibly a whole lot of Art had rubbed off on me.

A ship should not ride on a single anchor,
nor life on a single hope.

— **Epictetus**

Chapter 10

UNCHARTED WATERS

Three months went by before I heard from Art. One day I received a letter from him at home:

> *Dear Samantha,*
>
> *A few days ago I came close to living your fantasy of swimming with the dolphins. I was doing some snorkeling off the side of my sailboat when I spotted about two dozen of them heading straight for me. I tried to act naturally, making no gestures that might scare them off. Just when I thought they were going to swim right up to me, they veered slightly and kept a safe distance. I immediately thought of you and felt it was time to write. I've actually missed our meetings every month.*
>
> *Like you, I developed a real attachment to them. I want to emphasize something I said at our first meeting. Commitment means persistence with a purpose. I hope over your first year in the job I have clarified what commitment really means. It means you have to persist in focusing on what's important. Otherwise you lose sight of it. You have to persist in leading by example. If you*

don't, your example is not what it should be. You have to persist in rewarding success. Neglect this and you are not fully capitalizing on what success can bring. You have to persist in managing disrespect. Otherwise, disrespect manages you.

And, the same applies to improving things. You can't rest on past success. You have to continuously look for a better way. Never stop learning or challenging yourself and others. Finally, you have to persist in taking risks. Doing all of these takes courage. A lot of it.

Let me end by saying I hope I never gave you the feeling what we talked about was easy. It's an ongoing challenge. It takes someone like you. Someone with the courage to commit. The spirit of commitment means you strive to improve. Looking for a better way means coming up with a better set of the eight principles you need to sculpt your own art of leadership. Living that way, lovely lady, is the power of total commitment, the legacy of a leader.

> *All my best,*
> *Art*